MOUNTAINS OF
THE MOON

MOUNTAINS OF THE MOON

Greg Kuzma

STEPHEN F. AUSTIN STATE UNIVERSITY PRESS
NACOGDOCHES ★ TEXAS

Stephen F. Austin State University Press
P.O. Box 13007, SFA Station
Nacogdoches, TX   75962-3007
sfapress@sfasu.edu

Manufactured in the United States of America

LIBRARY OF CONGRESS IN PUBLICATION DATA
Kuzma, Greg
Mountains of the Moon / Greg Kuzma

p. cm.
ISBN: 978-1-936205-63-9

1. Poetry. 2. American Poetry. 3. Kuzma, Greg.

The paper used in this book meets the requirements of ANSI/NISO Z39.48-1992 (R1997) (Permanence of Paper)

Typeset in Garamond

ACKNOWLEDGMENTS

"The Wish," "Flowers," "My Father's Deafness," "The Knife Without a Handle That Never Had a Blade," and "The Boulevard" all appeared in *The Midwest Quarterly*.

"Funeral Poem for My Father" appeared in the anthology *A Good Man,* edited by Irv Broughton and published by Fawcett Columbine, New York, 1993.

"Lunch Break at Vien Dong" appeared in *North Dakota Quarterly*.

"Treasures of the Czars" was performed on National Public Radio.

"The Precautions" appeared in *Crazyhorse*.

"Having my Asshole Cut" appeared in *Green Mountains Review*.

"The Rain" appeared in *The Massachusetts Review*.

"Kissing in the Car" appeared in *Hurākan*.

For Jeff, for Barb, for Dad, for Jax, for Mark, for Alex, and

for all the thousands of my beloved students

"Mountains That We Moved."—Bob Seger

CONTENTS

THE RAIN

It's raining, I sit and listen. Go
out, let it hit me, walk out to the garage.
I scare up a stray cat, bent over the cat
dish, he kicks the bowl with his foot, slides
back as if to run into a corner, then makes
a dash for the open door, runs past me, then
is gone. He had to run towards me to get
away from me. Is this some principle? Is
this what my son told about, tonight on the
phone, going to the doctor, wanting the
work done, not wanting to be put off? He
wanted the surgery, he wanted it done right
away, while everybody else would sit and talk.
Of course they rescheduled him for another day.
He wanted the pain, if that's what it would take.
And then he had it. It hurt. Putting the
shots in, that was the bad part. Now he
peels off the dead skin. Imagine waiting
for cancer to come back, we said. What must
that be like? Having it, then facing it,
then having it gone, then waiting for it
to come back? Or come back in a new spot?
Is that the worst thing there is? I thought
about that for a second or two, having offered
my own view now and then, only to be proved
wrong. Thinking I knew about death, then
have my brother die, a whole world opened.

Then to run from it, as I remember running,
actually running in the hot sun, trying to forget.
Was it only in turning towards it, like the
cat wanting to run from me, then, at the
last moment, turning to face me, running
straight at me, for whatever I might do?
And then I came to stop running, and I
turned around and walked home. This is
where I live now, and the rain falls.
All day we worked in the yard, my daughter
and Barb, Jackie and Barb, let me say their
names, trimming bushes, cutting away new
growth, hoeing up weeds. It was my
rest day, day to write poems, do papers,
write letters. But I could not resist,
hearing them calling to each other across
some happy distance, or saw them carrying
their tools, how happily they ran from one
thing to another, scarcely done with one
thing that they did not start another.
Happily I went to join them, sharing a
cigarette, giving some advice, actually
went into the bushes near the black-raspberry
patch, and pulled some big weeds. How
beautiful the weeds were, and thought of
some alternative universe where they are
honored, but pulled them up, and carried
them, wanting to contribute. All day
the rain threatened. A few drops at
ten, and then a partial clearing, then
more clouds moved in. I put the sprinklers

out on the new grass, walked around, drank
coffee. Everywhere were heaps of things
discarded, new young trees that had looked
to get a start in the pfitzers, which my
daughter cut out. She walked right in
wearing shorts, and snipped them. I have
a picture of her carrying one, like a big
corsage, or a magic wand, completely intact,
upright, and all its leaves upstanding, not
yet wilted. Down by the street I found
the new grass, only just visible, sprouting
from the seed I spread last week, coming
up through the straw. And when I turned
around, to give up and stop my running,
there was no one there, no one in hard
pursuit as I had thought, and came and
walked home. And this is where I walked
to. Now a soft rain falls.

THE WISH

It has been my whole life. Once
was born in me that hope which
even now sustains me.
How last night when Mark called
so confident and everything, I smiled,
I held the phone hard and long.
I listened hard and long. Who has had
so many struggles, so many disappointments,
still I did not close my heart.
I remember, as a child, reading a book,
holding it, I wanted the world somehow,
I wanted to hold the world like that book.
Which later I understood to mean that
I wanted to write a book. But I have
done that, and it did not matter.
I have a whole bookcase filled with
my books. I have them facing out, so the
full covers show. The newest one with its
wonderful reds and yellows. That's not
it. That's not what I need. It is The
Wish I need never to die.
The Wish must live always just
beyond me, just beyond my reach.
We are all like this, are we not?
The part of us for which there are
no words? The part that dreams at night,
those incoherent eloquent garbles,

like two nights ago, the fish as big as
a suitcase, and the water a few inches deep.
It swam around and around at my
feet, I keeping the line tight the whole
time, as my father taught me.
But it was hard to keep it from
tangling itself among the chair legs.
I was fishing in a classroom, the
room had six or eight inches of water
on the floor, which I did not find
unusual. It was The Wish talking,
running the camera, feeding me my lines.
Then the fish dropped off, and I woke up. In
the car I feel it so strong. I get the door
closed, put the music on. I think The Wish
has written the music. And then I listen to
it—hundreds of things flash through me.
It's like I'm inhabited by energy. The
Chopin tape is a language of beauty. But
there are no words. I keep trying to find on
my tongue where a sequence of notes will
become language. Then I arrive
home. I am young again.
My mind clear. The world beautiful.
I have been with The Wish. She is lovely
and has long hair that washes over me.
I have to roll the window down to let her hang
out. We are like two dogs, two puppies, we are
so enthusiastic. Yeah though I walk
through the valley of the shadow of death,
she is with me still, my rod, my staff,

my comforter. After Jeff died I could not find
her. The world was empty. They had gone off
together, the two of them. Finally he let her
go. And she came back to me.
One night, at the Doane College Library, she
returned. Together we wrote the poem.
I remember picking my feet up to run to the
car, I was so excited. It's all good now. She
spends time with me every day.
Coming late sometimes, toward afternoon,
or just before bed, like last night, reading
myself down into a stupor. Then, my light
fading, she sat beside me, helped me turn
the pages. There, where I never would have found
it, she showed me the story of Ian Tyson and the
miracle of his new work. I who had loved
his folk songs, now am given this
new mission. What will they be like?—I
wonder—these new cowboy songs of his?
I tell you now my friends, The Wish is
beautiful. She is like a mountain stream,
the waters rushing over the rocks. She bade me
follow her into the current, feeling her chill
fingers along my legs. She bids me
see where the water turns white like a rush
of thoughts, or like my heart near to bursting.
There where the water changes from gold
to that deeper green, some magic flash—is
it a shiny stone?—the silver side of a trout
turning?—my hand goes out to touch,
to reach. That is when I fall in or wake up,

dazed, gasping, still in my bathrobe, miles
from home. And then I hear her
laughing at me.

THE AMAZING CONCOCTIONS

return to me now in sunlight—
sunlight on the old back porch—we
had not torn it down yet—
sunlight on the table where we worked—
a card table, set up in the yard beneath
the maple tree, light that draped one
side of it, the other in shadow, as with
the prow of some ship into the wave,
gone under, and crowd back further into
the light. And I am there, where I
do not know to go, where I have
not ever gone before, into the
town of time, my yard on
Schuyler Street when I was six
or eight. And there beside me
who? A he or she?—the
light will not disclose, the spell
will not reveal. More coffee in the
cup, please—give me another jolt,
Kim—some more cream too—
I see I am out. Light opens
like a rose into the shadows—
a porthole looking out onto
the sea, the wild waves and
sky, which opens further to
let me through—and I am either
out or in—I can't decide—
but back where I was. Beside

me someone stands—obedient
assistant, in a print dress—
fresh as the light itself, or
is it coveralls?—no matter—
we are at work. I have
my mother's glasses out of
the cupboard, one with blue
tint, maybe a wrinkled skin,
into which I pour the orange juice,
nearly to the top, then set it
out upon the table top. We laugh
at that. Such a big glass of
juice. And how long a day to
follow that with, and how
many things to do! But we are not
done with it yet. Out of the pickle
jar we fish the lunker lying deep
and green along the bottom, amongst
black pepper corns and other
aquatic presences,
and slide it into the glass
of juice. It settles like a whale
into the depths, lies catty-cornered
in the bottom of the glass, one
side pressed towards us, but the rest
receding in the orange eternity,
cucumber submarine surprise—
imagine Father on his way to work,
a little rushed, to see it loom up
at him out of the depths. Now
in a tall and slender glass, where
we have seen them in the happy

house, cracking ice the whole way
up, like some internal skeleton, or
specimen, amidst much fanfare and
exuberance, bottles of liquor
amber on the sideboard, or
crystal gin so crisp and cold
in some shivery blurred glass,
we dump in rocks instead and
then pour in the lemonade,
but not way up, to let the rocks
protrude. What shall we call it?
we ask—gunk on the rocks, or fog—
to imitate the famous names of
drinks—which did our parents in
one night when they get in towards
midnight, stumble up the stairs, cry
out in new-made voices, their animal
cries, the grunts of wild
predicament—but who, in
the midst of a waterfall of laughter,
can turn to me quite sober and
exclaim—"Are you having a hard
time sleeping?"—then tuck me
back in bed again—after which
their giggles resume, a bubble
like a pot of eggs. In memory of
that, in tribute to whatever they
are, fools or toads, we giggle along
with the next glass, doing the mad
concoctions while the sun broadpetaled,
folds around us her endearing arms.
Put another pickle in she says,

until we fill the glass over the top
and juice pours down over the table.
There, that does it! Grass goes into
the next glass, handfuls torn out, and
we are both on our knees tearing it—
Mom will be mad to see the stains—
and stuff it all in. Inside the house we
get the liquor bottles out, heavy and
swollen with significance, from their
secret dark, and dump one in—
then chicken out and put the bottles back.
And what is this?—brown rain on
Saturday, or Muddy River—No—
The Malarky, we say, for Mr. Malarky
across the street, on his mat upon
his knees over his precious grass,
cutting out dandelions. And carry it
out, and lift it up, presenting it
like someone in a movie of The Grail,
knights in armor, drinking toasts
in a hall, after to smash against each
other—so we do—putting the grass
concoction down—then bumping into
each other till we fall. Now in the
bottom of the fourth glass I pour
a handful of marbles, cat eyes,
onto which the stale 7-Up in the
bottle with the funny contraption of
a cap, a clamp of metal with a
rubber cork, which Father says
never works, sipping the soda—
so we sip it, make a face, then

hold it to the light to see the cat
eyes looking back, out of the depths,
but no cats, mysterious, turned every
which way, looking for their cats
perhaps. And set it on the table with
the rest. Into the next a drawer of
Father's bolts over which we pour milk
out of the fridge. Then a piece of mint
from the garden, floating
on top, as we've seen Mother do.
The table looks festive. Each to their
special drink to come there, lift it
smiling, drink it down and change—
like Dr. Jekyll into Mr. Hyde—pour it
down then quickly tell a joke—even
the quiet one who does not speak—
grow playful in the aftermath. We
look down into the depths—what
secrets there? What mysteries to
probe? Sunlight looks with us,
its arm around us, where curling in
the orange the pickle-snouted fish
is sleeping or the disembodied cats
stare back and will not scare. Now in
the next we pour from the spigot side
of the house plain water onto which I
launch my little boat, to bob about
each time we tip the glass—then
move on quickly to tomato juice on
top of motor oil, which then change
places in the glass a drink with
stripes—until we have them all out

in plain sight, a vast array of
festive drinks, all colors of the sun.
Who would we be if we drank this?
What would it make us say? And
pick it up, and bring it to our lips,
even the motor oil, then turn
transformed or with a new resolve,
older and wiser than before or
then with dignity stride off three
long and measured steps until
we fold up in a heap beneath
the maple tree. Mother came home
and rescued us, where had she
been all day?—before we hurt
ourselves—then like we always did
veered off to go some other way,
played War the rest of the afternoon,
shooting each other to death repeatedly,
falling in heaps then getting up again,
only to fall once more, until we
could not get up anymore. That
night for dinner Mother made
amazing pot roast which I always
loved, complete with wheels of
carrots and the great volcano mashed
potatoes with its lake of gravy spilling
down like lava down the sides
over the puny villagers below.

FLOWERS

Spirea is first, before columbine.
Is spirea a flower? It's a bush,
covered in flowers. There are good
years. Sometimes it's all white.
Before that red buds bloom. Or
is the lilac first? We have three
flowering crabs, graying red in the
leaf. All the energy goes
to the blooms. It's quite amazing.
Later we will kick the apples
all summer, slide down the hill
out walking. You can roll on
the round fruit, the way the
pyramids were built. They slid
the big blocks along over the
stones. I have nothing of that
scope in mind. Just to keep track
of the blooms, not to miss too
much. Lily of the valley is in
here someplace. I have a wild
patch that grows out onto the
lawn. Which I mow back, though
this year I got down on all fours
and dug a couple dozen up. They're
all interconnected underneath the soil.
It surprised me. The mechanics of a
thing are always new. You get used

to the surface play of light,
the shape of the little bells of
white, and that fragrance. There
I was, down on my knees, humble,
glad for the work. These little
useless projects are what join us
to the universe. The patch was
moved back, close to the house.
Over the year I'll probably forget,
and then next year, in spring again,
it will be a blessing unlooked for.
We have some ornamental plums as
well. Are they before the lilacs?
I don't know. And the pear tree,
covered this year, but no scent.
I was out tonight to check the pears.
We have maybe two hundred. Some of
the fruit are false, or stopped.
They've started to shrink back.
Nature is so clean. What doesn't
get a chance to grow falls, or is
swept away. Maybe rabbits eat the
dead fruit. Myrtle is early too.
I think I saw those bright blue
flowers through the snow. I was out
getting in the car, going off
somewhere, in a hurry, like I am.
I caught the look of a flower, and
it stopped me. Where had winter gone?
And I not mourned? They're still
blooming, through it all, though some

strange other ground cover has
joined in, and rises up above it
in the same patch. Which the bees
love. Barb will yank that other
nameless stuff, and throw it on
the lawn. We are careless gardeners.
Still, the ground's intact. It
has some driving sense of what it
does. Myrtle must be first. No,
there's another one, a little
orchid that comes up in early March
I think. It pushes through the
snow. No name for it either.
What a beauty! Now the poppies.
With the cool weather and the
gentle rain they are flourishing.
I never do a thing, I never even
look to see what's happening,
and then there are a hundred on
the hill. Beside them the peonies
bide their time. The ants cover
the buds, coaxing them out. Iris
are here too. They smell like
grape soda. Now we have some
daisies in the new garden. Next
to the spot the lilies were, which
I dug up, and moved around the yard.
I was feeling brave that day. They
all survived, though I was hard on
them. Digging and cutting through
some of the roots. So I felt

connected to the earth, making a
few deft changes. Someone will
see them years from now, and wonder
how they got there. I have a whole
new row of them all the way out
by the alley. You can hardly see
them from the house. Yet, if you
walk there, they are there. The
yard is full of phlox back by the
trees. I never touch them. Where
they come from I can't say. I
never do a thing, then there they
are. The yard tonight was full of
scent. It nearly overwhelmed me
when I got from the car. What had
I done to deserve them? Who had I
been kind to? Not myself, certainly.
I hated myself all day, all week.
Going about, my head hung down,
grumpy, disagreeable. Then I
drove home and found the flowers.
Early too, in the lawn, the violets.
They're so short you have to look
hard to see them. A couple have
drifted over and planted themselves
in our garden along the driveway.
Beside the garage. When they came
there I can't say. I just live here.
I go in and out. Talk on the phone.
Some days, like today, I can't do
anything that pleases me. Tried to

put the sprinkler on the new seed out
front, which promptly came apart and
squirted me. My glasses were all
rained on. Everything I did today
was like that. Mock orange
is blooming out in front, on the
hill coming up. That's a scent
that is not forgotten. Which do
I like the best? Which do I need
the most? If I had a choice, what
would I plant, if I could have only
one? Any one would do. Barb's
got daisies in the garden too.
They've been climbing every day,
their stems stretching, their
buds growing fat. Yesterday I
saw them blooming. So, what do
I do tonight? Worry about my class.
Get the poems out, and worry. Look
over the work for tomorrow. My
stomach will be turning over.
Sweat on my brow will form. I
have no seasons. I am always on
call. My stems are wiry and tough,
and always reaching, always out of
reach of what they need. I have
no flowers. Just dark foliage,
brooding and confused. Winter or
spring, summer or fall, I carry
myself along, yanking up my roots,
tugging at the earth. I am never at

home, never at peace. Forsythia I
missed this year. Did it bloom at
all? Those were lost weeks. Later
in the summer the day lilies will
come. We've a big patch out by the
road, which you can see from your
car as you drive by. Look
at them. Stop. Get out of your
car. If you see me out walking,
aimless, far from the house,
make me stop and look with you.

MY FATHER'S DEAFNESS

It was the imperfection of him
taught me the world. More than
anything he could have done or
said. Now I narrow in on the truth
of it. It taught me loss. How much
is intended, but how little gets
through. As when we would speak.
Reducing our lives to but the simplest
things. To make him hear more you
had to shout. To shout meant you
were angry or worked up. So our
best memories are of squaring off,
face to face. When confronted by
your complete intent, and hearing
every word I said, he was in control,
he knew what I meant. From this I
learned persistence, how you had to
go at things over and over, and hard.
Left alone, to drift out of earshot, he
would wander off, like a toddler,
get all wrapped up in something.
But to look at him, full in the face,
shouting. Then he would say,
so quietly, as if it were obvious,
"I hear you." How much can be
taken in with the eyes? His eyes were
good, the finest eyes. Was why he

looked so hard at me when I was near
him. Holding my mouth in his eyes, as
the deaf do, reading my lips. While I
thought all the time he admired me,
enjoyed my company. How much can
be done with a glance, how much
love can be conveyed? Left
alone he would close down.
Close his hand around a file,
around a hammer, and work.
He was great for working. Not
just because he liked it, now I
realize, but because once he was
working he could not be expected
to talk. He was safe there. Involved.
Doing something. Not having
to fail. And to think that all this
time we thought he liked it, how he
hid away down in the cellar. Or I
remember him washing the windows.
Standing the storms against the walls
of the garage, then going at them. In
my memory that's what he's always
doing. Washing storms. When I wanted
to play ball, or go fishing. What did
he see there in the glass? Reflected
back, the strange, distorted image of a
man, to keep him company. Where I
would not. Or I see him making soup.
Nothing great. Just Campbell's in a
pot. With his back turned. He would so

often turn his back, which meant he
did not want to talk. It took me
forty years to read his signals.
Now, were he alive, we would
make a good team. I could tell him
what the world wants, and he could do it.
I could be his translator, and turn
the mumbles of the world into
deeds. But what if what I wanted
could not be said? What if what I
wanted could not be shouted,
for fear of embarrassment? So have
I given you my childhood in three
lines of a poem. While silence
deepened in the house. Deaf, he
did not go out and argue with the
peddlers as his mother had. Deaf
he did not sit in the bar and play
cards, catching snits of conversation,
rolling his lip, kinking his eye to
catch a sudden flutter in a player's
hand. He was not one to search out the
stock exchange, or enjoy drawing
rooms, where you swam or sunk on
how quick you could get something
said. He was a reader. I say that now
in trepidation. Always with a book, a
bowl of peanuts beside him, which he
would reach out to absently, and
play then with the fingers
of one hand. Cracking a shell.

But maybe he did not like reading.
But pretended. Opening a book
to ward the world off. Pretending to
be involved, when really he might not
care. Oh but what wondrous things
he knew. Late in his life we would talk
a bit, and something would come up, and
he would say, "Do you know about that
guy?"—the one who invented the
locomotive, for instance, or swam The
Channel. He would ask my
permission, ask if I had the time,
and then he would tell the whole
long wondrous story he had absorbed
through his eyes. Not hearing words
well spoken he did not know how
to say them. Mother would say,
unkindly, how he murdered the
English language. And I will not
forget, and squirm as I say it, how
he substituted "organism" for
"orgasm." In a sentence about a
woman who wanted an "organism."
Many were these, his monstrous
coinages. And once in a college
class, I used his word "assumations,"
which had a nice sound. I was hot
in the midst of some point I was
trying to make when the teacher
said—"I know of no such word,
assumations"—and I knew it was

his cursed word, to dog me all my
days. I blushed and hid in my
chair, and did not talk again.
Those weeks were my father's
life, in miniature. But I did not say,
if this for me, then how much worse for
him. Which I say now. For the good it
will do. Noise did not bother him. Or it
did, and made him more deaf. But he
could stand it. Stand it because
he could not hear it, and
so accept louder noise, which
made him more deaf still. To this
day I identify him with noisy things.
He had a terrible chainsaw, a
real monster, very heavy, which we
made run one summer. Or the saw
in the basement, the circular saw. When
it was spinning, no one could talk. But
when it was spinning he knew what to
do. Wreathed in sawdust, cutting wood,
blinking the dust out of his eyes,
he was in his glory. Or
I remember how he held the chainsaw
taking it in both arms like a squalling
baby, letting it have its cry, his face
relaxed, as if he paid it no mind.
But held it gently so as not to make
it worse. He accepted machines.
He suffered no ambivalence. Whatever
was wrong with them he fixed as if there

were no other choice, then fired them
up. Then in the roar and the smoke
he stood there, as if just
born of that fury. Deaf, he did not
cringe, or cower, as I would, shielding
his eyes or ears. It was his
posture of fearlessness and
equilibrium where everything was
as it had to be, in perfect harmony.
Everything he liked was noisy.
He had his guns. We got into
muzzle loaders, and set up the
archery target, and walked off down
the road until we could barely see
it, then load the big Plains rifle.
He liked weight and mass, lead
and steel, and packed the ball in
tight with a wad around it, torn
from an old shirt. We did it all for
the "report," that roar that started
with the spark of the cap, the fizzle
of powder, then the growing storm, and
then the slam of the ball flying, like
the loud slap of a heavy door. What did
he hear? Just the loud bang? But it was
a confirmation, a cry of life.
Each thing had its voice, however
harsh. Which he could tolerate. Which
he could understand, and forgive. And
what of the trout, gasping on the bank of
the trout stream, mouths wide? What did

he think they said? I see him in his
shop, at work, among the men,
all the lathes and grinders going,
moving among the machines, wearing
his apron, tending them, as if in some
strange garden, touching the oil can
to them, slaking their thirst. I went to
visit him there once or twice, in the shop
of machines. You couldn't talk.
We walked around, meeting the men.
It was so loud. Each man had his
machine, stood by it smiling, as in
some weird marriage, arm in arm,
the gray cowling of the lathe, the
gray work shirt of father's friend,
and in our ears that wild music of
steel. Mother said the shop made
him deaf. An injury first, falling off a
barn, and blood which broke
through an eardrum, so he started
off deaf in one ear. I remember that
expression, his "good ear." How
he would turn his good ear towards
me—which was it? Left or right?
I do not know. Or nights my mom
would complain of, how he would
put the good ear to the pillow and
the deaf one up, tuning out the
world. His deafness hurt him, but
he used it too. Far from the house,
doing a job he liked, when mother

would call him to come in, to do
something he didn't like, he might
pretend not to hear, and go on
working. I cannot verify the truth
of this except in my own life, playing
the same game like my Dad. Or
times we would argue, together,
late at night, he could turn away from
me and let those last words go,
the words I should not have said,
to let me take them back, and
then we might resume again.
As if they had never been said.
His deafness said you could not hear
everything. His deafness said you
could not know everything. His
deafness said there were conditions,
as in his favorite expression from
Shakespeare, about time and tide
in the affairs of men, when things
might run perhaps in his favor, or
when he was "out of commission."
Was it moisture in the air that
hurt him? The days he could not
hear, but would stand at the sink
and make a fist, and lay his fist
on the sideboard. Or he would have a
cold, which settled in his ear, and
deafened him. And I can still
remember his huge motions of
trying to throw off the cold, or

wheezing in a handkerchief, how
heroic he seemed, caught in the grip
of gigantic forces, forces that for
all his thrashing, he could not hope
to vanquish. A pall of doom
hung over him, of something
irreparable, some deep harm we
could not understand. But it had made
a cripple in the world. And how he
lived in that pall, accepting it, and
yet with sadness. There
was a melancholy about him, that
went with his deafness, that partook
of his silences, and fed my own
depression. Long would I sit
in my room and hear him, moving boards
in the cellar, and the strange muffled
sounds in the wall, like
some blind thing, a mile in the earth,
or a ghost in the attic, moving boxes,
trying to build a body
or a life. Year by year his hearing
got worse. Until he could not hear at
all, and when Jeff died and we went to
the funeral home, stood in the room as
if what had happened had
happened to someone else.
And I envied him the illusion,
that it was possible not to know,
not to feel, but to be insulated from
the truth. And I remember going there

in the car with my mother, though they
had been divorced for years, and he
going the wrong way—perhaps
he did not want to go?—
and she trying to wrench the wheel out
of his hands, as if he had always gone
the wrong way. Towards the
end of their marriage he used his
deafness as a weapon. She would
have plans to go out, and needed
the car, but when she was dressed and
ready to go, there he would be
out in the driveway washing it.
He did not want her to go. He
did not want her to leave him.
A few years ago he bought a
hearing aid. We had been after
him for years to get one, but he had
always said it would not work.
It worked! I talked to him and
he would hear me. It was amazing how
much he heard. But I, so used
to yelling at him, would keep yelling,
until he would reach out, and put
his hand on my wrist, and say
"You don't have to shout. I hear
you." A whole world opened to
him. Where before the house had
been quiet, there was the TV on,
some crazy show, and there the two
of them would sit, my father and

his brother Bill, or watching
their movies, night after night.
Or you would watch them going
up the street together towards the
plaza, to shop, and you could see they
were talking, just ambling along,
exchanging platitudes, the very picture
of content. Maybe he'd
hear the birds singing on such a
walk, or the wind recite a little
of its poetry, in the blossoms of
his hawthorn tree.

DRUNKS

We are not perfectible.
Jackie's fighting with her roommates.
Ten months, and she wants to move out.
Twenty-one, and just a birthday, what?—
two weeks ago, a big party, the house
rocked all night, the beer flowed.
You can't live with drunks, I guess,
or people, who, when they get drunk,
don't know who you are. A note on
the counter causes a huge rift:
"Thanks for cleaning up the house,"
she writes to the one who worked,
the other finds it, pouts,
crumples the note. There is all
this weight of the unsaid.
Sitting with her at The Union
she is full of outrage, full of
resolve. She speaks with a
new-found courage. Pushed past
the point of ever going back,
she is free, free at last. Or
she imagines it. The view is good
from here. She has climbed to a
high point, high on a ridge,
above the tumult, the wind
sweeps her hair. I like the
way she crosses her arms. It looks

like she's decided to hear the case,
come into the room she's turned into
a court, to hear the presentations.
What can they ever say? A party
every night, even on school nights,
the whole place trashed, drunks
trying to get into the bathroom
where another drunk's blockaded
himself. Some push
on top, the others on the bottom
and the door buckles. Late,
in the parking lot, the guy
who just drank up a fifth of
tequila, flashes his knife
around. Sober, he's polite, a
little goony, likable, comes over
to borrow tea bags. Inside every
person another lurks, to turn
each hallway into a dark alley.
Conversations are hopeless. Words
are tar—you get your tongue
stuck. Pretty soon there's
no way out. The best way
through is just to drink, the
more the merrier, the quicker
the better. Pour yourself two or
three shots. Try to catch up. But
what if you have homework,
a test at dawn, a teacher
who doesn't know the world exists,
except the book he wrote.

I saw her papers in advanced news
writing those desolate first weeks. A
slash of red across the top, words
bigger than I've ever seen,
except on sweatshirts—NO! or
DO OVER!, and then a hundred little
crabs of red gnawing at her sentences.
Anything that sits there on the page
and doesn't run they move in on.
Two pages into the story
and there's nothing left. A nice
thing to take home, carry in her
book bag. To open the door and
come into the smoky house. It's
party time! The TV's blaring,
the Cosby Show, dishes in the sink
from yesterday, phone messages
scattered about. Somebody's left
a cigarette that rolled off the table and
burned through the carpet. The plant's
tipped over. Cigarette butts in the pot
used for an ashtray. Now Scott wants to
dance. He's impossible. They all are.
What night is it anyway? So you tear
through, break away, grab a moldy apple
from the fridge, and run. So many
strangers, laughter and the loud
TV. Everybody smokes. Already
there's a grocery bag filled to
the top with cans. The fridge
has the same old head of lettuce,

beers jammed in on every shelf.
Their blood must be all beer now.
Then you're out the door. It's
calm in the hall. The party
like the tide has not come out this
far. A distant surf pounds on rocks.
Soon it will spill out monstrous
in the hall and down the stairs.
Mark went through the window by
the door, and someone else tore off
the banister. Next day to wake up
groggy with a splitting head.
What did you say last night?
Where did you go? And maybe in your
bed someone you've never seen.
No money left. A dry throat. Sore
gums. Somebody' s puked on the rug,
and there's a string of puke across
the floor and down the hall.
Better not touch anything. Tiptoe in,
tiptoe out. The body curled around the
toilet is alive, it moves its foot.
Beyond the foot a leg you recognize, a
pair of shorts, a shirt—YOURS!—
the one you just bought
for your birthday and were saving—
the face familiar but horrible,
it's Dawn, girl of the morning,
woman of the New Age. Isn't the
rent due? Where's the phone bill?
No one knows. It's not yet time

to be alive. You go into your
mother role, the pose that Dawn
can't stand. These last few months
even when you know she's overlooked
the obvious you just won't tell her.
The card she bought and should
have sent in March, a month late,
poking out from under dirty
underwear. You're sick of it!
It's time for the showdown.
Burned out cigarette butts at six
paces, buckets of warm beer drained
from all the orphaned cans and
derelicts, with cigarettes snuffed
out, a nice brown stain to the mix,
splashed in a face. Or maybe she
should drink it? Pour it down her
till she gags. You have your list
ready. All her offenses neatly
written in. A date by each. In
your memory each one branded there.
So this is what apartment life is like.
Housekeeping with some other "young
adults." Steph screaming into the phone,
hating her father, running to her room,
slamming the door. And
what are your offenses? Are you
without sin? Maybe they are tired of
being lectured by Miss Perfect?
Always with somewhere to go, a busy
schedule, people to interview.

And that time with the phone where
you could not hear your person on
the other end for all Dawn's shouting.
How afterwards she pouted and got mad.
Maybe they just like to inconvenience
you, upset the neat arrangement of
your day? Irked by your lists, with
everything in place, each item scratched
off when complete. How you always
take yourself away, as if you're better
than the ones who stay behind. That's
the reason that they waste themselves
night after night. To prove to you
it never can be right, your nifty
life, with everything in place. We are
not perfectible. We live halfway
between the angels and the beasts.
Smoke cigarettes and ruin our lungs,
drink beer until we die of thirst,
study till our eyes go blind. We
hate our fathers, or is it our
mothers we hate? And if the world
wants this or that from us, we tell
it to Fuck Off. It's a great story.
Twenty million stories like it
acted out night after night.
Come morning the survivors gather,
marry, and the vans go out to put
them in their houses. Even Dawn will
marry, quit smoking, find a job she
likes. A child will come to her, as

if by accident. She'll
want to keep in touch. A letter now
and then. Remember those great
parties out at Meadow Wood? How mad
you used to get? All those great
fights we had. Remember when?

FUNERAL POEM FOR MY FATHER

I have one hammer. It is somewhere.
My other one, made in China I think,
with a black rubber handle
I loaned my daughter for her new
apartment. The rule is—when you don't
know how to use things, give them
away. She doesn't know how
to fix things either. She and her
roommates have a kitten. It is a joy
to hold it, and to play with it.
Its favorite thing is crumpled
paper on the floor, balled up and
rolled. With crumpled paper and
a kitten we can play all day,
and go to bed tired at night, tired and
fulfilled. Let the house fall in around
us, let the roof fall in,
our hammer is missing or we can't
find it. I think I saw it
on the porch, or it was in the
drawer last week, last year.
Where did I see it last? Or in
a dream? I don't know how
to fix things. All I know is how to
break them, or wear them out.
My pleasure is to wear my shoes right
down to the threads, and then,

when they're exhausted,
let them rest. My father's pleasure
was a different thing. Equipped with
every kind of tool, he waited for
the world to break. He knew it
would. He had seen it before. He had
buried a son. Friends would come
from here and there, as they have
come today, and ask of Harry for his
expertise. Mike told me—or was it
Sue?—you could always rely on Harry—
just bring him your problem—
give him time—and he would
have an answer. Toward the end
he liked being so treated.
Don't we all like being relied on—
somebody with an answer—
amidst the million questions of
our lives. Can it be bolted?
he would ask, and answer. Can it be
tapped or threaded? Can it be filed
down if it is too big, or hardened if
it is too soft. We are all
too soft, I guess, in need of
proper tempering in the furnace
of life. Put a wire on the back
and we can hang it on the wall,
and look at it. We have a picture!
Check to see by scraping with a
penknife through layers and layers
of paint—to see what sort of wood it

is, and if it is cherry, like this
casket here, or pine, the way we used
to bury men on the frontier—
mountain men—whose stories my
father knew—if it were wood like
that, but not oak!—he did not
quite approve of oak—presto
in six months or maybe in a
jiffy of a year—we'd have
a piece of furniture—a night stand
or a dresser or commode—standing
startled in its own raw wood, bright
beneath a window sill. My father
knew how to do things—
he knew things, and how to do things,
in order that I could idle myself
and worry endlessly on how to say things.
His house is filled with things
done, but not done with. Touched
into life, where the hand passing
over the wood over and over
discloses and brings out the grain—
so that you look at it and it offers
itself as it is, without disguises.
So a tree lived and grew and stretched
to grow in the light, which now
encloses my father's socks, safe
in a drawer. And which will serve
my feet, now his socks are mine.
So have his tools passed to me.
More hammers than I have ever

seen, except in a hardware store.
A dozen different shapes. All manner of
handle and head. For tapping, for
nudging, for setting, for pounding
nails, for pulling out the ones I
can't pound straight. Can there be so
many jobs to do, I ask, so many which
might be done exactly right,
precisely, the way he knows? So
many things that need to be persuaded.
Now these hammers fall to my hands.
The rule is—the tools set down by those
who know their use fall
always to those less competent.
Just as the rule seems to be
that all this steel that lasts
forever would mock our lives
for being so brief. I know
that I will never know the
things he knew. I know that
I can never live so long enough
to know the secrets kept by the
metal, or held in the grain of
the wood, disclosed as it is by
his hand, revealed in his eye.
Father, your work is done. We
will all pick up where you
leave off, the fisherman to fish, my
son to carry your rod and reel, or
bang his knuckles on a bolt fixing
his car with your wrench. The poets

to write. My daughter sits at the
table in your house tonight as I
write this, and writes her poems. My
wife consults the undercarriage
of a chair to see how you
joined fabric to wood,
and how you placed your tacks,
and plans how she will keep
your memory.

THE PRECAUTIONS

Valentine's Day, 1992. Rain in the
Midwest, the yard looked wet, leaves
had blown back in from where Mark and
I raked them and mowed them up. Work
that never gets done, that needs to be
done over and over, of the long journey
that cannot be accounted for, for which
there is no finish line, no prize, no
trophy at the end, and we are forever
in training, eating breakfast in a rush,
drinking coffee in a rush, and coming
home to bed, to crash amidst images
of dreams, parallel stories of some
endless journey, and waking once
again with more to do. More poems to
read, more papers to assign, more poems
to write, and now and then a holiday
to organize our thoughts. Today is
love's day, yesterday we were alone or
lost between the syllables, and I was
panicked in a moment in the car, and
turned the tape on to connect myself
to something I had known before, Hayden
Carruth reading his poems, and stopped
and bought some popcorn, and said hello
to Reed, the popcorn man, driving my car
from station to station through the

darkened chaos of my day, to finish out
the week of school in some accustomed
pattern of coherence, like wearing the
same shirt over and over, until I was
sure of the way it felt, and wanted to
go on doing that. And then it was Friday,
and the day of love, but worked all morning
at The Sportsman Bar, reading
book reports from class, trying to get
a moment free entirely for myself, like
taking the harness off the horse to let
it run free once around the track, just
for what it felt like, being both rider
and horse, being the wind in the mane,
and the rain that fell so lovely to the
ground. But it was safe inside, and I
tore through the manuscripts, marking and
praising, giving what I needed back, giving
to others that very thing I needed, and did
not get, giving and getting being confused in
my mind, and if one did not get what one
needed one might educate the world to what it
was, and did the whole bunch, all
except one long paper which in class had
slid across the desktop and knocked my
coffee over in a splash, whose front page
was all awash in coffee stain, and the
paper hard from being wet, hard like
the cover of a book. And I loved
what I did. Loved the work, and Jeanne
put her hand on my shoulder where I sat

in the booth and bent to my labor, and
rubbed my back for one ten-thousandth
of a second, just enough to let me know she
liked seeing me, had come, perhaps, even
against her will, to enjoy all the space I
took up, taking over a whole booth and
getting there by ten on Friday morning, to
sit all day and work, while in and out the
other patrons came and went, sitting there so
long I couldn't hardly stand
to walk down towards the bathroom three
or four times during the afternoon, having
had my fill of coffee, and then more,
thirsty and looking for another gulp of
energy. The papers were great. Oh, all
the usual little confusions, which I could
clear up in class the next week, but liking
what I read, and being glad that I had thought
to ask. Was asking the same as loving? And
making the students read their books of poems,
knowing it was good for them, loving how I
could sit by and watch like
a proud father, those first few hesitant
steps into the unknown. And then it was
four o'clock, and I was meeting Barb. We
had our valentines out on the table at
home, and Barby brought her vase of roses
back from school where they had wowed the
multitudes, and I had my bag of gifts to
open. Was this what a Valentine's Day
was supposed to be? Standing in the

kitchen of the cold house, reading cards
in our coats. Barb's was the funnier card. It
shows two people on a couch, holding hands,
and one is thinking, oh say it, say those
three little words I love to hear
you say—and then, inside, they're standing
at the open door and the husband is
saying "Let's Eat Out." As out the door we go.
As out the door we went, off to Lincoln and
Grisanti's Restaurant, treating ourselves for
what?—the third time this week, until it
seems almost a duty to order, until even what
makes it fun seems like an effort,
of the same things over and over, of the
same hunger opening like a rose inside
us, and carrying it around as if it were our
gift to the world, or what connected us.
We put our name in at Grisanti's, then
walked across to the health-food store,
there to while away the time. It was filled with
amazing things, bins of interesting grains, beans
of all kinds, mixtures of snack foods
and dried fruits, pasta made of soy and
garlic and cilantro, spaghetti made of
artichokes, and over against the wall, in
the fresh produce case, chard and mustard
greens like the wealth of nations, and lovely
tortured-looking beets with stems of leaves
partially attached, and fresh organic carrots
looking small and introspective, dark in
dark skins, but one of my students was

peeling some in bowls at the checkout
counter, emerging under her knife like
essences, the purest orange, the brightest
flash of steel, and hers the whitest hand.
Barb found some great pasta with a label
printed in German, and stood there like a
kid puzzling it out, saying the words aloud,
then wrote it all down to share with her
students. I was so hungry I wanted to
buy everything, and peered deeply into
jars of salsa, trying to see what it was
made of, and shook the packages of soup
mix, hefted the jars of fruit jam prepared
without sugar, and marveled at all the boxes
of spaghetti made from different things, and
finally bought some dark rye spaghetti,
heavy and looking like the soil in our yard
after a rain, and marveled at the mind of
man for all these satisfactions I had never known.
I could sit all day in the Bar and drink coffee
and nibble at my toast, being on a
diet, or sneak my bags of M&Ms in, keeping
my blood sugar up, and never yank a carrot
from the earth, feeling the long tap root
tug at the soil, or all the little hair roots
it is nourished by. Or when I saw the big
bunches of greens I lifted them, and felt
the weight of the rain in them, and
somewhere in me deep arose some deep
and ancient hunger. It was getting
expensive, this walking around waiting to

be called at Grisanti's, and every aisle I
went down I found something else, something I
had always wanted to try, or something we had
eaten once but almost forgotten, like tobouli,
which I always used to make when the kids were
small, and punish them with it, telling them
how the world did not always taste sweet to be
good, and all these long years of forgetting,
not even heeding my own words, but
sucked my candy by the handful, keeping
my blood sugar up in the rain at The
Sportsman Bar. I who had a streamlined
life, simplifying what I ate, to concentrate
on words and write new poems, and not
be bothered in the kitchen long hours,
making something no one would eat,
but was awakened, seeing a bean
assortment for chili which looked complex,
all colors and shapes of beans, and even had
barley and red lentils, and bought
that. Over at Grisanti's we got our table,
amidst the throngs of lovers all waiting
to start their evenings, and I remarked
how every party was a party for two,
and looked to see how pretty the women
had made themselves up, and how
handsome the men, for this was love's
day, of a whole long year of forgetting,
or getting lost, or working for the sake of
work, or driving my car in the dark from
outpost to outpost, getting saved a little in

the dark, or hearing Hayden's voice to guide
me home to poetry again. All around us the
lovers ate and drank, and now and then at a
nearby table materialized a young man
dressed in formal wear, and
sang a verse or two of some pretty song.
Halfway through our meal he came to
our table and stood there, and took
from his pocket a little round harmonica,
and blew into it, which made a sound I had
not heard since junior high,
when we were all forced to take music, and
set the pitch for himself, and sang us a
love song. Nothing else eventful happened. I
did not make a speech, or profess my love,
or give to Barb a diamond ring, as I had
done two months before in this very place,
just across the room in a corner booth,
on a quiet night, when the
waitresses flocked around to look at it.
Love is expensive, gesture and symbol,
proof and enactment, and patient too,
for Barb who waited twenty years for
her engagement ring, and we who are fat
now, and fighting our weight, who tire
easily and fall asleep on the couch, and
who are always eating out to save on time
and energy, and always rushing to get
through the day, until to crash at the end.
And is there time for love, amidst a
million distractions, and a million new

ideas for poems, for projects at school,
for problems that need to be solved, for
movies at the cinema which we have not yet
seen and so have not passed judgment on?
What movie would we see tonight?
Or would we go with our daughter
to the bar and watch her boyfriend's
band? Which we had never seen
before, or heard. The Precautions, which
Barb calls The Percussions, which might be
a better name given how loud they are. I
could not decide what I wanted to do, but
slipping always into the easier thing,
easier to go to a movie, and buy a ticket,
and talk to the ticket girl as if she were
a friend, and buy our popcorn and pop, and
feel connected to the world, and
then go in and render our
opinion, all those millions spent, all
those dozens of people involved, and
two days later in trying to tell someone
what movie we saw forget the title, forget
the plot, only to recall I did not like it
very much, but cannot say why, and not even
take time out to advise
my mother which movies we did like,
but sliding along deeper into forgetfulness,
deeper into the headlong rush of our
lives. What is there time for? And is
there time for love? And who is this
boyfriend, anyway? Or a bar I've never

heard of in The Haymarket, where
young people gather to drink and dance.
And when was it we were last young?
By some accident we went to the bar. Kris
drove, whose husband Dave Penley plays
drums for the band. And Kirstin, Jackie's
roommate, of the golden hair. At the door
they took our money for the cover charge,
just as if we were anyone, or young
still, and we went in and
took our places at some tables in
front of the stage. Everybody was
drinking beer and smoking cigarettes.
The juke box played songs I had not
heard before, and very loud, so that
it was hard to hear. Members of the band
stood around beside the stage and talked,
and people I did not know moved around
inside the room as if there were places
to go, destinations, distances to
conquer. Jackie told us that Evan was
very nervous. Evan is the lead singer,
Evan Rail. And I kept seeing him
appearing and disappearing off in the
shadows, the way I used to pace back and
forth in my office before class, trying
to get the right momentum to
go in on, trying to shake off all the
doubts, or remember my lines, or walk
a little further in my body, hoping it
would start to fit and feel natural, so

I could be at home in it. Was nervous to
have us here, Jackie's Mom and Dad,
two music critics from "The New York Times"
or "Rolling Stone," and I who had
written all those reviews of poetry
during the eighties, and had hardly
ever been pleased, what would I think
of this, on a Saturday night in the rain?
Around us the tables began to fill up.
Strangers came out of the dark to talk to
Jackie. People I had never seen knew our
daughter. And one big guy with a good
build kept brushing past my chair and
nearly knocked me over two or
three times. At last the music started. The
band assembled itself on the stage, plugged
in their instruments, or whatever it is they
do, and started to play. It was very loud.
There were no apologies,
no introductions. There was no framing of
intent, or other readings to refer to.
Just a wave of music, or a wall, a rush,
and then Evan's voice, fighting the
tide. Barb sat beside me, but she
seemed far away. The floor shook,
and the table also. Tremors in the
floor were tremors in my feet, tremors
in my feet shook my bowels, and my
ears were assaulted, and I could not
think. Barb turned to me to speak,
and spoke—but I could not hear a word.

And I spoke to her, but I could not hear
what it was that I said, and do not know
what I said. The wave grew in fury
and assaulted the shore, followed by
another wave. Atop it, buoyed up
by it, swept along by it, kept afloat in it,
Evan's voice rode the wave, argued with
it, tried to lead it, tried to follow
where it led. He seemed both victim of
the wave and master, both the wave's inception
and the shore on which it broke. Ahead
of it he seemed to shape it, beneath it—
it rode over him and nearly drowned him out—
nearly crushed him as it seemed it would
crush everyone. I had never heard
such loud music. "Heard" is not the word.
I did not hear it. I experienced it. But it
was not even that. It fought me for my
consciousness. It seemed to want to occupy
my place at the table, or drive me from the
room. It seemed to want to
take over my body, take over my mind,
replace my endless mutterings with its
own mad impulse. So this is what my
students do, I thought, after dark, after
I have poked and stirred them for an
hour with poetry. Taking refuge from
their cares in the midst of the storm,
just at the edge of the eye of the
hurricane where the winds are most
strong, where the swirlings are most

powerful. And saw a student from a
class of mine sitting very calm where
again and again the wave broke. The song
ended, and another song began. Another
large and shapeless, monstrous yet not
malignant, an endless eruption of notes
and cries, and the same heroic riding of
the wave, Evan alone in the middle of
the stage, leaning somewhat crumpled
against the microphone. Later, driving
home, I thought of the special quality
of this music, how it mirrors perfectly
the world the young see, the chaos
all around them, the immensity, the
power greater than themselves, and their
own small way within it, through the
midst of it, or riding the wave itself,
which might shatter them and all their
hopes, fearful—for who would not be
in the midst of such violence?—yet bold
too, standing up to it, letting it wash
over them, hoping perhaps to steal
some power from it or perhaps its secret,
as Evan stood, seeming to find his voice
in the voice of the onslaught. It was
hard to take! And I remembered my
summers with Barb's family at the shore
in Delaware, how obsessed I became
with the sea, and body surfing, feeling
the immense power of it, and being
buffeted about, or twisted, nearly broken,

on a bad run, but then to rise above it
just a little bit and coast in all the way
to shore on the wave's crest. I was
forty and discovering the sea!
And walk back, stagger back to the
house, my bathing suit full of sand,
my hair full of sand, as if driven into
my skin by the force, and stand there
in the shower, in the hot water, sipping a
cold beer, feeling fully alive. It was a
night like that. The sea had grown
an arm and come inland two thousand
miles. The sea had found a metaphor
in the music of the band called The
Precautions, and a lone brave surfer
to ride the crest of the waves named
Evan Rail, or bearing sometimes perhaps
my own name, as somehow in the
midst of all the fury I emerged a bit
and rode the music in. The songs
I didn't know. Nor did it matter
what the words were. It was just the
human voice, now at odds with the music,
now together with it, arguing with it,
dancing, singing. Now and then a phrase
came through the noise, and
my mind clung to that phrase and
grabbed it like a piece of cork or
ring buoy, and hugged it to myself
and rode with it in towards the shore
that did not quite ever arrive. And

then we were dancing—Jackie first,
and Kris, both wearing red for
Valentine's Day, and Kirstin in red,
and the men with mustaches who had
hunched around our tables, standing
and shaking. And even myself,
caught in the current and swept up,
forgetting my awkwardness and my
objections. Three or four times we
were out on the floor, like venturing
out into the surf at Rehobeth Beach,
clutching our frail little rafts, or
standing frail and naked in our
bodies. Out on the floor the fury
infected the dancers. Shoulder and
ankle, wrist and neck, muscle and
bone shook and snapped and popped.
And once Kirstin drew near me in the
onslaught, and brushed my shoulder,
then spun off at a dizzy pace like
some loose electron. And here was
the fat girl I had seen sitting for so
long, fluid and loose in the music
utterly transformed. And our son
come late to the bar, out on the floor
with his sister, wrestling with the
monster of the sea. It was wonderful to
see them there, the two of them,
holding each other up and yet not
touching, moving almost in unison,
victims and masters at once, I could

not tell which they were, as on and on
the band played. Evan was in fine
voice. We remarked later, Barb and
I, how truly lovely his voice is,
standing painting woodwork the next
day, talking about the band. They
call themselves The Precautions.
What the name means is another mystery.
They're back at Oscar's next weekend,
both Friday and Saturday nights, for a
return engagement. Maybe we will
see you there?

THE BOULEVARD

We lived in the same house
but in different rooms. Mine
faced to the front of the house,
on Schuyler Street. Tall spruces
towered upwards past my window.
In the branches birds sat, nested,
and beyond them a lone walker,
walking a dog, or a child on a bike
right out in the middle of the street—
no cars coming, to get off and stop
to fix her chain. We played ball
there, on Schuyler, hitting into the
overhung limbs of giant silver maples,
and in the autumn Dad raised up a
huge leaf pile into which we leaped
repeatedly, a kind of water made
elastic and with a pleasant smell
like old coats. Old Man Malarky
kept the house across the street.
He was sixty, maybe eighty, kneeling
on his lawn. He'd work all day
digging dandelions, as if that were a
thing to do. Until at last one green
stood out, a wedge of it,
a band, unflawed, perfected. The
mail would come, some time in
the afternoon, the mailman turning up

the short front walk, then rising up
three steps to stop, then slide the
letters through the slot. Some bills,
a letter or two from Grandma
in New York, then some more bills,
news of the world, like clockwork,
once a day except on Sundays of
course. Things were, if possible,
even quieter then. I would sit
at my desk where voices were
what birds seemed to be saying,
or the spin of bike wheels when
children passed, or maybe Father had
the sprinkler out, whirring and
whirring and getting nowhere, until
the grass was good and drenched—
then move it to another spot.
Weekends in the summer he
would trim the hedge, and I
would lie back on my bed and hear
the snip-snip-snipping of the blades,
the click when the stops came together,
the sound of his rake over the fresh cut
stems, or now and then the scrape of its
tines on the walk. In winter, when
I was small, George Paige
would clatter bottles on the porch,
bringing milk, and then, summer
come round again, the clip clop of
the horse down Schuyler Street,
the popcorn man in his wagon.

He had a little coffee pot filled
with melted butter, would pour it
thick upon my corn, and then a thick
cascade of salt, then clip clop down
the street headed for Franklin Field
and evening softball games. We
played mumbletypeg
on the front grass beneath my
window. Going through all the
stations, even the ones that were
hard for me—the head drop the
worst, where the jackknife had
to turn once on its way down,
and stick in the earth. The point
standing up on my head made me
nervous, then to watch it fall right
past my eyes. I remember scoring, how
the knife had to stick, but even if
it stuck it had to span, and you
would stick your two long fingers out
to make the width. Standing erect
with the knife atop your head, and
the whole world poised to see
what would result. That was
"headsies" I think, now
it comes back to me. In another
move you would cross your left
arm over your chest and grab
the lobe of your ear, then wedge
the right arm through to flick
the blade. Did we kneel for that?

Or marbles. We would play in
the snow. And Paul and I could
start just at the edge of the hedge
and roll them all the way to school.
And one day Paul showed up with
steelies, ball bearings from somewhere,
which I had not seen, until my Father
brought some home from work.
I can still see them in his lunch box, a
clutch of shiny eggs from some
bedazzled eagle, maybe the golden
one that sat atop the flagpole in the
park. Sundays we'd take the garbage
out, through the picket gate, and
set the barrels out by the curb.
For years that meant lugging the
ashes from the coal furnace out of
the cellar and up the stairs, Dad
on one side, me huffing along,
one hand through the handle, the
other stuck to my wrist, bracing
the lift. And then next morning,
early, hearing the truck come
through, the men yelling. I became
a poet. When given a chance I
put together sixteen years of
listening out that window, birdsong
and the whisper of the wind, or
sitting there at my desk, having
come in from a hot run, to cool
myself in some reflection of

my day—and hear the silence
wash back in again from Schuyler
Street. Words in the silence.
Birdsong, a flutter of wings,
and steelies in a nest outside
my window. Old Man Malarky
with his digger, sitting, kneeling
on his lawn in endless scrutiny.
Jeff's room faced out on
The Boulevard. Once it had been the
canal, where people in the
neighborhood dumped trash.
Then, filled in, ran dirt up to
the city dump, where Dad and I
shot rats and looked for things
to save. By the time Jeff was
old enough to know, the road
ran two lanes on a side, and
with a stoplight just behind our
house. You could hardly get out of
the drive most days, and Dad
there, head over his right shoulder,
looking back against the line
of traffic, fuming. It was very
loud. Cars always sped on The
Boulevard, but coming to the light
would downshift fast, gear after
gear, from deep in some fierce
metallic throat, and then the rip
of rubber as the tires skid.
Stopped at the light, a driver

would look around, only to find
another driver in another supedup
car beside him.
Then signal to each other their
intent by revving up or running
through the gears. It was a
constant roar, spring, summer
and fall, radios blaring, the clash
and clangor of different stations,
insistent and incessant noise.
Jeff lay there as a child
and soaked it up. Went early off to
bed as evening traffic, headed
off to drive ins, rolled in
at the light, or sped up as it
went to yellow there outside his
room. And then woke up to it,
waking perhaps to a sudden squeal,
the driver seeing that he might
not stop in time, hitting the brakes to
lay two strips of rubber with
attendant squeals, then lay two
more as he peeled out. What was
it?—the sound of progress? The
cry of the city? Growing pains?
Raw voices of vast steel engines.
The call of the wild, imperishable
road. It took off there for everywhere.
You could go north to the mountains
and endless rain, fishing and stars,
or elsewheres off to Utica and

bigger towns, more fierce storms
of cars. My room fronted on the
eighteenth-century, upstate hamlet
Rome, New York had been, Jeff
heard industrial rage and terror
at the wheel, the future revving
it up with the brake on, ready to
rip. Thousands of cars a day were
his symphony, while I heard the
lone single flute of the window
bird. They called to him,
through unruly numbers of themselves,
each voice to rise above another
with a terrible assertiveness,
then to be conquered by another
louder still. No argument measured
and tame, to guide by reason,
but by power and torque. Lying
in his bed like that, he married
the road, distance and longing,
speed and the burn at the heart
of it all, to go off in a terrible
fury of wheels, somewhere, nowhere,
anywhere at all, anywhere at all
but here. And then he was off!
Soon as he could he was gone,
telling no one. Then to return
in the middle of the night,
to crash and sleep on the couch.
He kept odd hours, a strange
impossible schedule, lived on

a bite of apple, a gallon of gas for
his Norton bike, a couple bucks for
smokes. He was always in motion,
or when not in motion,
stood like a wraith in the kitchen,
and poured himself a glass of
water at the sink, then disappeared
for weeks off into Canada.
It called to him, whatever it was,
turning his nights into days,
keeping him up all night racing
to get back through pouring rain.
Once he gave me a ride on his
bike, tearing up the road at
eighty, ripping through the gears.
Rounding a mountain curve I grabbed
so tight around his waist I thought
we'd both go tumbling off, but
felt then the tug of the force,
while banshee winds screamed
past my head and his. Getting
off I staggered, while he came gently
to his feet, as if just getting out
of bed after a good night's sleep. He
died on the road, as was intended
from the very first. The scream of
metal grating on itself, trying to
get free of gravity, or fear, or in
its mad attempt to leave the past
behind, shrill in his ears. To this
day still I cannot drive my car

without Jeff sitting down beside me.
Or I will see him, a lone biker,
coming at me 'round a curve,
coming for all he's worth, and
almost to collide, then zoom past me
off to anywhere at all. And a raw
terrible energy seizes me,
shakes me, shakes me, and
then lets me go.

KISSING IN THE CAR

We used to do it in high school.
With other people then. They had
the same parts, different names,
after eating bacon and tomato
sandwiches. I remember Dave Guido
in the back seat, with Sue,
while I made out in front. The time
with Kathy—we went to the dump.
I must have thought if we went
someplace dark enough, disreputable
enough, something unforeseen could
happen. We kissed and kissed
until our mouths were polished
to a sheen. Whatever was supposed
to happen I don't think I knew.
It was enough just to smell her.
All I could do to cross that gulf
between us. Oh the ache and
labored breathing, even now, thirty
years after, I ride the ocean swell
of that night even now. We had been
alone so long, untouched, the self
unseen, in secret in the dark. The
life we had—it was the life of
books, homework and algebra. Anything
beyond that veered towards embarrassment,
a furious red face. Some subterranean

self stalked us, some life within
that had not yet awoke, which like
the submarine on Saturday, in the
old black-and-white war movie,
ran silent, ran deep. And you could
scream in the dark, below the
untroubled brow of the sea, no one
would hear, depth charges blowing
all around you, then that dead-on
hit we dreaded. She had a face I liked,
I don't know why, a darker tone to
her skin, as if she always had a tan,
and a strange way of talking—in
evasions—as if with each
sentence you had to reply, you had
to prove your worth. Language itself
that vast roiling sea, where if you
came up for air, and threw the hatch
wide open, waves might pour down
in to sink you. Things said alone
and to yourself, could be murder
in public. Suddenly to send them
all packing, or off into wild wails
of derision. I could not handle
the split between outer and inner—
still can't—these words in your
hands now, even so—I fear your
catcalls and your boredom. Out
of essential shame—that I am
not you?—poetry came—or being
born too late, too soon?—which

was it? And I forever naked—
even if I haven't said it—give me
time and I'll get to it! Some poets
are clothed entirely, or in gesture
clothed, knowing always what the next
word is to be—while I blush
writing, fumbling with the buttons in
the dark. But who knows how
far you can go, or when to stop?
There was this beautiful age—
maybe fifteen or sixteen, when
everything was out of control.
Words did not work—or worked too
well. And you could get a door
slammed in your face! Even alone,
with the door shut, opening a book,
you could find a poem there,
a throb in the middle of the page—
or a throb of perfume down the
hall, growing in the mind to
overwhelm. What was it, this
ache? Partial knowledge, partial
glimpses, the strip of bare calf
over the top of her socks, so
beautiful, first love and preview
of the world. What would it be
to have that whole leg bare?—
or thrown across your lap?—no
one could conceive of it! The
heart pounding the whole time,
trying to get out, trying to stand

up on its toes and peek, beating
madly in its cage, wild animal
of the self, blind and furious, like
the red face naked where words
failed. We lived as in a maze,
people and places, bodies and
faces, corridors of people,
avenues down which we went
only to reach some end and turn.
I knew the way to Kathy's house, and
borrowed a bike. I got there tired,
and came to an abrupt corner of the
maze—she stood in the door and
would not let me in. Or walked with
Linda Vella home, holding hands. I
did not kiss her. That would have
to wait three years at least,
that kiss another corner
we would turn. Each life is a maze.
One way for each of us
that no one knows. And I pulled
Kathy up too hard on that dock
in summer, and would marry someone
else. And Barb Colella earlier,
I loved with everything I was,
only her name was right. We are all
the same people, I know it—each
and all with partial knowledge, partial
glimpses. Inside the same mad
heart, hands that reach out to touch.
And I recall that gentleness taking her

hand, or in the fall, the bus ride to
the game, the motor rumbling
like some deep aching, binding
us one and all across the lap.
Most everything I did was wrong.
Would step on her feet, dancing,
or knock her books out of her hands
trying to carry them. In close,
my face near hers, would make her
jump from the sound of my voice,
so loud, from trying to make my
deaf father hear. Did nobody
want me? Kiss me in the car and let
me know. Yet my life was mine. Each
setback endowed the future. Each
turn in the maze brought
me closer to now. I remember how
sharp the turns, until I thought my
mind rehearsed humiliations
endlessly. Now I see them as my
greatest moments. There was about
the past a wonderful excitement.
We thought that it would
all be lost—which was not true.
I know now all the chances everybody
gets. But it was only how we had
it wrong that life was good. The
more desperate, the more intense.
I didn't kiss in the car much.
Once or twice with Kathy, then
with Sue. Then, at fifty, last week,

Barb is forty-eight, we did. We had
gone out to dinner with Jackie our
daughter and her new boyfriend
John. I was just back from a reading
trip. Barb and I had missed each
other. There, at the dinner, I told my
stories, John felt good and talked a
lot, Jackie squeezed my leg, we
all got drunk. Here, if we could have
remade the world, I might have. Here
was my daughter for the sister I
did not have, John for my brother
reborn in another time, I was my own
father laughing. And Barb, the girl
beside me in the car, in the world's
good time. Outside, in the car
finally, alone with Barb, we kissed.
And did not stop. Some fever took us, in
its purest form, a wild confusion shook
us and we kissed. We had been
through everything together. No
mystery remained except that constant
mystery of what we are. Here were
the people who chose each other once
and who kept choosing, always with the
same result. We were both at the very
edge of—in the dark—some immense
fulfillment which already had
happened. And it was 1958 again, the
dash lights dim, our whispers like
a music in the dark, the traffic outside

like the sea sound breathing of the earth
itself. Beyond us the world shook and
shuddered as we trembled
in the presence of each other. Never,
I don't think, had I loved kissing more.

HAVING MY ASSHOLE CUT

Walt Gardner hears me out.
Sprawls in his chair,
relaxed, his shirt matches
the wallpaper.
He knows if I talk long enough,
if he hears me out, I'll start
to relax. He knows he'll find
out soon enough, eventually,
what's bothering me. He
knows he knows the stuff
that if he told me and I
studied it I never would
come in. I'd be as smart as
he is, my own doctor, doctoring
myself. He knows as well that if
I knew the stuff he knows, the
things the body does, will do, as
it disintegrates, as it falls
apart on its way to the grave, I
would not sleep at all, but lie
there stiff in the dark, my pulse
racing, feeling distant twinges
in the dark like twinkling stars
of horror, constellations of despair.
A little information is a
danger, but a lot? And if one knew
the whole truth, as God knows,
what would you do? You'd run

away like God and hide, unable
to show your face in company,
never to be seen again. To
hear them talking about Uncle
Joe who "sickened" and died,
which meant in fact the
cancer chewed him inside
out, ate through his flesh,
and how he screamed
week after week, crying "God,
what have I done? Why
have you forsaken me?"
These truths being self evident,
to him, and being to my way
of mind suspicions I invoke
on the strength of my neurotic
intuitions, the two of us
are never totally at ease.
After all, he presides upon
the growing decay of my
flesh, he witnesses
through all the many years of
our friendship, the graying
and the falling of my hair,
the slow erosion of my muscle
tone, and how, when
rising from my chair,
I come up dazed for the loss
of blood to my brain, which also
has a name, which has its proper
signature and mark,
set of symptoms, set of

causes, all plotted and
known, and I decay
before his very eyes, between
visits, slipping gradually out
of reach, until, at last,
nothing can be done for me, and
he will shake his head,
and touch my wife's or daughter's
hand. The doctor knows us
better than we know ourselves.
The stars of our journeys are
plotted on the charts of his
walls, and though he
fears no evil, and though he means
none, he must look and know
and see, nor ever turn away.
Like God he knows our
fears and faults, and for
our imposition on his peace
of mind, assesses grand
sums against our accounts.
What will this bit of foreplay
cost, I think, watching him
talk. How much time will he
allow for the creation of
that valuable illusion that
his learning exists just for us,
that he has time for us
and no one else? It is
a studied manner. Walt
used to blush in the early days.
He'd be shocked, I guess,

at what he'd gotten into,
something he'd said, or some
indiscretion falling from our
tongues. One hardens oneself,
learning to forgive, learning
the many faces of the truth.
And one could care a lot,
and be unlikable, or one could
be the sweetest thing, only
to die horribly, beyond the
healing reach of his hands.
You learn to let them go.
You learn to respect the
weight of life, the gravity
of dying. The earth
calls us home. We play like
children for a while, no
sense of limit or mortality,
and squander everything
like children will, and then,
suddenly, suddenly old,
suddenly stricken, it is a
wrong world. The trick
is to retain one's sense
of humor. He is, after all, only
a man. We are, after all, only
women and men,
children of time, spoiled,
impractical, and everyone's
a dreamer of some distant field
bathed in kindly light when with
a heavy heart the diagnosis

comes. Whatever life is,
it is not long enough, it
is not free enough from pain,
from care, from bills to pay.
And even when asleep,
we go to it for how we might
escape, our dreams are worse.
I was having a problem. Addicted
to coffee I would start
early and not be able to stop.
All day I'd drink it, and if
I didn't have enough I'd
stop on the way home, after
racquetball, and guzzle a
liter of coke. Without it I
could not think, or teach,
or write. The problem, if there
were a problem other than this
thing itself, my asshole hurt,
my prostate gland
and all the various assorted
regions near and surrounding
the castle. Until, at last,
after a whole day of belting
it down, I'd go to pee but
could not, or would have to
stand there like a fool with
the door locked, dribbling
in the pot. I was caught,
as they say, between a rock and
a hard place, between mouth and
anus, caught like the earth

itself, as it chokes and dies.
What goes in comes out, as any
doctor knows, as
any person walking on the beach,
walking over the garbage
and dead fish, holding their nose,
looking but trying not to see.
Infected, inflamed, it was getting
hard to sit, hard to think about
another thing. Then one day, in
the shower, after racquetball,
scrubbing between
my legs, my fingers catch the
edge of a flap of a thing,
growing on my asshole.
That's when the pictures flashed
in my head, of prostatic
cancer like Patton's armies
sweeping on big arrows out
of the gland, into bladder
and anus. Was this it?
Would I live? Was this the start
of a new life, a grotesque death?
And saw myself
with crotch sewn up, intestines
routed out the side into a bag,
and even then the daily
watch if cancer would
return. Who knew where
the cutting would stop,
once it began? Who knows
how insane the world is?

Living our lives under the sun,
doing our best to get through,
then sitting there at last,
on judgment day,
explaining the routine
as all around us the
assembled hosts, some
extended committee, blush
and look away, fold and
unfold their hands. "Let's
get this straight," the
doctor says, in charge,
"You drink two dozen cups a
day of what? Of this?"
And takes a sip. And
spits the liquid out.
Looks pass around the table.
Wings rub and scuff
against each other.
Then you know what a fool
you are, who broke the laws
of God and man,
now to be punished.
I wake from the dream. It's Walt,
slouched in the corner, looking
fresh, healthy and young. I'm
jealous. I wish we could trade
places, and he could fail to
write the poems and I could
overlook like God the wayward
flock. "Let's have a look
at this thing," he

says, and I begin to strip.
I'm sweating. I don't like
being sick. I don't like being
here, being old, and sitting in
a room with circus animals
all over the walls,
and then the other wall
whose crossed lines match
Walt's shirt. How did we
get to this juncture?
How might I unweave the
fabric of the life that brought
me here, undrink the stuff
I drank, uneat the junk I
ate, tear up the million
cigarettes I had to have,
one at a time, one after
lunch, one as I started to
saw the log, and setting it
aside, to take it up again,
one in the car, having reached
the car, having crossed the
dangerous parking lot, having
gobbled off another hour from
the clock, and so on, year
after year. It's 1981.
Please take me back. Get
me out jogging on the road,
eight miles a day, and build
the muscles up. But don't let me
lie in the sun when I get home!
No, don't let me roll over

onto my stomach, putting my
shoulders to the sky, the
shoulders that are spotted now
with burned skin. And that
iced tea I dreamed of, all the
last miles home in the heat, dump
it out in the grass, drink water
instead or fruit juice. Show me
the finish line just over the
hill, shaded in lovely trees,
where we shall win, where virtue
leads us through, and all our
wretched habits fall away.
Walt's got me up on the table
now, the good doctor, bending
over. I hear him click the
door latch in the door. This
is personal! Let me spare
you the details. I'm starting
to heat up around the ears. I'm
starting to feeling home again
and safe. This is
the way we dream of paradise,
held in the healing arms of
the doctor. No God in Heaven
to redeem this flesh, no
one else to probe and look, no
one else to isolate the problem.
Someday my soul will need
redemption, but today I'll settle
for a few quick shots of
Novocain in the right places.

I have a vision of him in a
welder's mask, the torch zapping
through. It hurts like hell.
That's how I know my fears are
real. That's how we know the
doctor is involved. No way
we could hurt ourselves
alone, like this. It takes
two, in this strange ritual.
This is how the healing can begin.
I shake his hand. I make a
joke or two. He makes a
better joke. Then I am
out the door, alive once
more, imperfect but alive.
No case is hopeless. In the
hallowed halls of medicine
we have seen much, we've
seen it all. Walt, I think,
had a good time. He even gave
me the offending tag of
skin, the little nub with
all its blood and nerves.
No part of the body is
superfluous, but that the mind
goes there, feeling around in
the dark. No flock too large
the doctor will not reach his kind
hand in under the throat to calm
the racing heart. I get in
my car and speed off.
The world seems large again,

immense again, something I
understand. What a great
way to spend an hour on Friday
morning. I'm ecstatic.
To celebrate I drive down
to my favorite bar, drag in
my attaché case, write some
poems. Donna brings me
coffee out of the magic pot.
A couple cups and then the
ideas start, in a rush, one
after another, like joyous
circus animals, like elephants
parading head to tail. This is
the way I like it, blasting
through, the far side of
the grave. I throw my whole
full effort into a new poem,
work a while, then see my
coffee cup is running low.
Donna comes along and fills
it up.

LUNCH BREAK AT VIEN DONG

As I sit and wait with my daughter
my father comes and sits down in my body.
He is dead a year and a half, but he is
on the move. Where has he been traveling?
Out over the poles, or along his favorite
trout streams. I have been on one of his
streams and walked for an hour without
seeing him, or anyone. Certainly there is
room out there for his journey. Not having
to catch trout now, or account for
the hours spent, not having to hurry back.
He walks adeptly over the slippery rocks,
but does not slip and fall, being cousin
to the dark, and all dark things his neighbors
now. Or does he fish there still, with one
of his wonderful fly rods, the ones he never
lived to use, casting the tiny fly like magic
onto the fast water. Do the fish come, allowing
themselves to be caught? An endless supply. And
a creel that will never be empty, no more a day
of getting skunked, or feeling guilty to catch
only a little one. Or lighting up a cigarette in
the old way? No longer worried about disease, or
getting short of breath, but drawing the smoke
in deep, the way he used to as a young man.
All things come to him now. The deer do not
flee, but browse along the stream, no longer

spooked by his coughing, or the slap of his
big rubber boots as he walks. What was
he looking for all those years? Can he
remember, now, he who has won the world?
Now he comes to reside in my body
back from his journey. I feel the sweet
fatigue of his body, and arms that still
sing from the fly casting. My daughter is
talking, of what I cannot hear. I have
drifted away a bit, my head filled with
images of the white water of the stream.
And now I lift my fork and pick up a delicate
piece of broccoli. I look at it as if it
were something I no longer need. Was I
hungry once, and followed my stomach around?
Was there something I looked for in the
world, something I did not have?
My daughter continues to talk. I pick
up my napkin, I bring it to my mouth,
I wipe my lips, and then I fold it
carefully the way he did,
and then I put it down.

A SUNDAY DRIVE

Does anybody take them anymore?
In amber light I see the figures hunch
and lean. One comes across the lawn,
scuffing his feet. They are all stills,
stopped in the midst of life, taking a
breath, having just taken one. We are
in time's pocket, the lint of history, index
of lost attributes. You can tell by the look
of the clothes they have just been up to the
attic, ransacking boxes, one trying to
wedge into old shoes, two sizes small.
And one brings in his hands up from
the cellar toy chest that little boat
we all chased after Christmas once.
Or hugs the teddy bear I had beside
my bed, the fur worn off around the
nose from nuzzling, the tongue a little
petal sewn on cockeyed. Young then,
fluffed and puffed. Out back the traffic
swallows hard, catches its breath,
will not go mad for fifteen years or so,
the road a narrow blacktop ending at the
dump. Outrageous lilacs blow
in their profusion at perimeters,
as if to guard these souls—
but let the light in anyway to
fade these photographs, yellow the shawl
thrown over the couch. This was that

world. All I did not know—like someone
else—another self who lived inside but
never talked, not even once in a while
disclose his meanings, as when the
caterpillars came—pharaonic army
like the sea itself—and how
we squashed them he and I—
an endless army of their plenitude.
So that made two of me, myself and what I
did not know to feel, surprise on
the face of the morning, and then
there was the self I kept the secret of,
such as what I really thought of cream of
mushroom soup—and one day let it out,
and marched around inside the house
singing how I hated it. That person
punished, sent upstairs. She used
the poisoner's method of dilution, a tiny
bit upon the spoon each day, until I'd
built my tolerance, until today I love
it fiercely, almost angrily, the can
on the shelf the same as forty years
ago, perverse time capsule. Inside,
I do not doubt, some twisted
self sleeps curled around his spoon,
or waiting to erupt. How many now is
that?—what is the toll?—
to make the family large enough?
No loneliness did I feel ever. Even
before Jeff was born I never missed
him. Only when he died did the ache
start. Come run on tiny feet to

fall up the steps of the old porch, made
of wood, sagging in the spring. And the
box elder tree I used to climb, one wide
fork near the ground, to get a leg on,
then pull up, be tall like them and see
into the heart of things. I had no body
except to fall, then was always rising
up again, reborn, joy's jumping jack, to
one day bounce to school and
stumble home. Dad was
building the cupboards then, would hear
him in the cellar with the hoarse cry of
the saw another friend. In it
two voices sang, the one against steel
teeth, the ring of teeth that lightly
clipped the guard, then the push through
wood, its yielding, bent to his whim, its
biscuit Yes. All week he cut steel,
to then come home to wood. And he another
one for sure, the father in the basement shop,
and then that other one he was to sit
upon the couch at night, still in his
work clothes, pouring the beer out of
the Schaefer quart. What strange elixir
that?—to soften the horizon of his mouth,
make him more quiet still. Another person
to pull at the heart? The mother
indistinct. I can't make her out.
But see her swishing down the street
on heels, her skirt flung out ahead of
her, then whipped right back again,
a strange contraption like a sprinkler,

to teeter homewards on her high opinion.
How many do I count for her?
The one who washed, the one who ironed,
the one who cooked, the one who talked.
Hearing now her voice calling
my father's name, still possessed of hope,
looking forward to another day, saying just
do this one thing more and we
can rest, and go off for a Sunday drive?
Is it recorded somewhere, in some seismic
shift of love's long aftershocks or
pattern to the pulse of love? I'd
like to see the way the needle jumped
and inked the graph, week unto week,
and months to years on towards the gradual
extinction of desire. Or have on tape her
early voice, still brimful of the morning
of that hope. I am in the
zone now of the amber light, hallway
dark of the house gone barefoot
for a drink, some midnight, lying there
to cough and wake in one of those
delicious fevers we are forged in,
mother standing by the bed, the glass
of water tepid in her hand. Faintly
soapy from my bathtub play. Then did we
cut the tree down as the baby cried, and
the worms fell out of the sky,
and saw my father burn them with his
torch, their snapping tents, the curling
fiery worms. Then did the Japanese beetle
shine in the palm of my hand, bejeweled

thing, such beauty to be hated so.
Beetles demolished the elm tree every
year, and father waged a war against
them, jugs of gasoline filled with
beetles like pennies glinting in
the bottom—nozzles and sprays, the thin
leaves chewed right through, the sky
beyond so blue. I am there with
them now, having wiggled back through a seam
in the cardboard box I made a house of, no
tongue in my head yet—when
was the poet born? And this
the smithy shop that forged the poet.
Heat of that lonely fever to melt the mind's
iron. All those thousand nights to sit
and watch my father busy with his tools
so to be made the fool of words,
to give each dumb thing voice—
in that house where everything went wrong.
So do we come to pity the past for its
helplessness. These who bore us, in their
terrible innocence, proclaim
their stories now, who never spoke a
stanza on their own behalves. Father
thought each question a trap—perhaps it
was, then mother's harsh particulars, no
afterglow of poetry, hers like my
father's, hitting the nail on the head,
driving it in flush, even as the wall of
the house they built fell down.
The world was beautiful and doomed,
the way we cut the worms in half—

a yellow custard ushered forth.
Late in the play that breaks the poet's
heart, while meaning nothing to an
audience, the father gets a line or two,
full fathom five, and staggers down the
stairs. Shakespeare singed his tongue,
words that grabbed the throat of morning,
words into deeds driving the car all
wet with dew. Putting the heater on.
We are from all things, indebted to all
things, even the cow pies in the field near
the stream sang to me. All these actors
without lines, actors who cannot remember
their lines, and no one there to write
the script in time. Six or eight of us
then lived in the house, maybe ten,
counting the imposters we never knew
till later who they were, and the poet
himself, the biggest imposter of all,
who stood there in the shower of his
words—a shell like armor, catching
the painful light of his life.
Language sprang up in the beetle's
copper shimmer in my hand—for oh
you had to tell that somewhere so it
would not be lost. Or in the sawdust
underneath the saw, the cardboard box
where Father caught the snow of the
boards he brought the final winter to.
Every Sunday we would go for our
ride. And get all twelve of us at
least into the car, all the wrong

people and names, the wrong name for
the flower beside the road, the
empty carsick feeling which I later found
was my desire—just the bud of it emergent
in some cold spring, was it
ever to bloom?—as heat went out of
the passion I was forged in, slammed
together in my mother's womb, and had
to put on coats of all colors and
shapes for how chill the world turned
out to be. In a green car we went forth,
green as the earth, bulging as cars
of that era did, as if with second thoughts
stricken, and might utter some brilliant
phrase, but mostly farted out the back, all
this to establish the terrible present,
ransacking the toy chest of the probable,
clutching my cap gun, hoping to see
along the road something to shoot.
We had a 49 Chevy, a truly beautiful
car, all green, deep and dark, with a
sun visor that hung out over the windshield,
and wheel skirts on the rear. Whitewalls
Father took the SOS pads to, to brighten our
motorcade. The seat cushions were a sort of
plastic weave, a kind of plaid, comprised
of thick fibers wider than threads, and
seated straight across you could
get all the family there, I wedged
in between father and mother,
for how I came between them, to reconcile
them in their odds and ends, as

they say children may, or poetry can, but
comes too late to save them from themselves.
And head out with a clang and grind, Dad
shifting the old style column shift,
a bundle of shanks and levers, a sort
of northwest motion being second gear,
and then to the south for down and—
was it back for third? Would go into
the country, having had our fill of city
life, to maybe get free of it all, hoping for
some new perspective. We liked to go up
by the lake, as I remember, through fields rocky
on both sides, swaying with cows swaying, and
maybe would have to stop while farmers
led their dazed pale sheep across, while I
got vaguely carsick or got out to pee. As
I feel nauseous now, lonely here and far
from home. Or they would stop for me,
to let me run out in the bushes by
the road—was it to play?—or did I
think to run away?—leaving the
two of them, alone, just for that moment,
as they would shortly let each other go
for good and ill and evermore, these two,
two wretched lonely lovely broken souls.

THE YOUNG

I love the young...
I do not love the old.
Oh, I love the old too,
and I will forgive them everything—
but it is the young I love.
Among them I am alive,
and the whole world lives in
their eyes. Walking past them
in the hall, I would like to jump
on and ride the way as kids
we'd grab a bumper on the icy
hill and let it take us all
the way to school. Amidst shouts!
A snowball tossed after us.
There is a current in them—
a white roil of water over
the rocks that would bruise them
and they glide among them or
even against the current itself—
poised there as on a wave coming
in a thousand miles of beach,
to move if not with the force
but in some happy tangent,
then leap from the board they
are riding, and take a soda pop
in hand! The old are tiresome,
endlessly so, made cautious

through error, their eyes burrowed
deep in the face, like a bear in
a cave far back from the light,
and have to be coaxed out—
as at a party I draw out
from the deep hollow of
the tree of them their thin
line of ants—slow and in a steady
single file—their small display—
is it?—of vitality, their army
of midgets. While all the time
beside us, the fountain of
Elizabeth erupts in a tower
of speech—the water roiling,
the boil of her tongue in the
pot of her head—steam issues
from her ears—is she going to
explode—or fly into orbit?
Or just stand there, poised as
on the threshold of immensity,
the narrow board of her perch,
taming that vast ocean of
herself. How young
Liz is, Barb says, as we rub
out the sleep from our eyes,
sit in the car for the drive
back. The dash lights coming on,
the tone so soothing. Yes,
it is good to get away from them
even a moment, catching our breath—
dying. All the way home we

die in the car, having let go
of her hand, the throb of the
young heart leaping. We get
anxious coming home—has it
rained?—did we leave the
windows open? And that bill
we did not pay? Or did you
pay it? And what about the
roof?—my surfboard on the
downward slope, a war whoop in
my throat—and they will do
it next, the young! Roof
surfing is next, and Mountain
Dew will be there, scanning
the heights of Chicago, letting
the wind whip. Our weekend is
long, as in a kind of preview
of eternity, our feet in tar,
our tongues grown circumspect,
a little piece of gossip stuck
between two teeth. Outside the
ancient earth rehearses endlessly
its own death. Leaves have
collapsed from the hackberry out
back, and over the brow of the
house one tree has slung its
sleepy arm. So does the soul
limp in exile here, far from the
kingdom of the young. Our
banishment complete, the laundry
done, the money stacked like

towels, tomatoes from the
garden packed away in jars,
hostage as we are to time,
draping our chains across our
backs, trying to get close enough
to kiss. Is it farewell?
Back Monday at school I park
my car in a rush, put up the
sunscreen, tip the coffee cup.
Then enter the flow of them,
the current north and south,
up past the courts of Harper-
Schramm I go, mingling the
whole way, stepping in and out.
All tiredness leaves me, my
years fall away, I pick up my
pace. At the end of my arm
my briefcase lightens—I
who could barely lift it out
of the car, past the tracks
by the heat plant I go, more kids
coming back from class than
going, taking the full light of
their faces into my face, the way
depressed people may sometimes be
restored, staring into bright
lights. Into the second block
they have made me young. The blocks
melt under me. Each step I take
is back in time, and by the
corner of 14th and Vine almost

expect the girl in red to greet
me, the guys there
put their arms around my
shoulder, whisper in my ear.
Or quick throw me a pass as I
break for the parking lot.
Restored I skip up the steps
and am home, among them now
invisible and indivisible.
No one laughs at my gray hair
or points to the stoop of my
back, no one remarks my dated
clothes, out of whatever life I
lived once, and got old in,
nobody calls me fool. In
the hall later I watch the old
leave, one by one, their worn
step on the stair, the way they
bundle up their clothes around
their throats—I who had not
noticed the wind! I who had been
baptized by the rain. Or watch
them group together,
frightened in the river of the
young, to make no sudden move
or lose their place, thence to be
swept away. And hear their grave
tones, the deep edge of concern
and disapproval in their voices.
Traitor to my class,
I cannot look at them, ashamed

of us both I guess, but stand
to watch the young bunch up
before the doors—and Jen comes
down and sticks her face in,
Jo stops by, leaps off the water
ski she's piloting, hands me
a page of something she just
wrote, is gone then in a wall
of light. Something undaunted
in them, something that has not
been sold, keeps their faces
clear. I am in love with them.
Uplifted by them, held in their
esteem, buoyed in the dream of
the young. Once I was old and
worn, much did I travel in the
dark beneath the earth, and was
a demon once, to stew in my own
black pot, a creature of scorn,
but then one day finding no
hate in me, they reached their
hands to lead me to the light.
Where does it start, this
joy they are possessed by? Being
a match for the world, strength
to its distances, patience to
its dull delays, come out
from the very birth of time.
Two nights ago I saw the
river at its source. It was
at McDonalds Restaurant, we

stopped there late, a young
girl took our order. Dark
beautiful skin, dark rivers of
hair flowing, and turned from
us to look away and laugh. The
object of her look we had to
rise up on our toes to see.
In a tiny car seat an infant sat,
strapped in, who almost overflowed
the seat. The mother got our
drinks, busied herself across
the counter, turning every now
and then to catch the eye of her
little one. When the mother
turned away the face of the
child went blank, the eyes flat
and empty, the mouth, toothless
as in old age, empty of all
expression—almost a mask of
death. Then would the mother
turn, emitting perhaps a tiny
cry, inaudible to us, as if
with the swing of her shoulders she
reached out to embrace the child?
Then would the face open, the gape
of the mouth become
the lantern-grin of Halloween,
the clown's perfect look—to flare
across the face while the eyes
leapt and danced and the whole
body shook! Here was the source itself—

opening in a room towards midnight,
the whole earth dark around us
miles and miles. May I not forget
them all my days.

TREASURES OF THE CZARS

Napoleon might have cautioned us—I can see
him pacing, "Don't go," he says, remembering
Russia in winter. Perhaps later, after it
was over, that snow stayed with him. The
earth and its repudiation of his dream. I
love snow. I remember my Northern birth. It
steadies in me, would draw me home. On my
Father's side we are Russian all the way
back. People of the snow. Barb keeps trying
to line me up with my forebears. Dreams,
herself, of travel. Like Napoleon, would
march me off to Moscow. The best of
intentions hers—a little opera, flash our
jeans around Red Square. Not
an invasion, by any means. We mean
them no harm. Maybe she wants
to leave me there, and cure my restlessness.
Why DO I write so much, Napoleon myself,
planning my next campaign? Something in
me walks these winter nights. I love the view
from outdoors, the house in the snow like a
great ship stewed in light. To peer through
windows frosted, great crystal chandeliers
inside and people wrapped together in the
presents of their bodies, dancing. Russia
haunts me even here, southwest of Lincoln,
1995. I can drop a century in a blink, drift

back, wrapped in furs we come on through the
drifts, the horses steaming, my version of
"Jingle Bells" in Russian playing on my
headphones. No trip to Russia this year. The
country in chaos again, traditional, a stormy
people, the language itself heavy and harsh, a lot
of cabbage and potatoes brought to a slow
boil. Too much vodka numbs the tongue,
deepens the vowels. The closest we can
come is Topeka, three hours off. It seems
a miracle. How did they get this show!
Maybe no one wanted it. We set out,
two-ish, the sky gray. Snow falling for
hours already, coats the ground. Yesterday
seventy degrees, I walked to The Union in
my shirtsleeves, bought a coke. Today it's
Russia, 1895. The Czar calls us. We go.
Travel is iffy. Tanking up we put in the
Puccini tape. It sets a nice desperate tone.
What a friend calls "whining," those
wonderful laments. When we get there
six hours later, having been frightened to
death, Puccini is hoarse, his tenors flat,
sopranos played out. Outside the storm,
inside, reciprocal, the heart cries
unaccommodated on some dingy stage.
Barb had heard about the show. Somebody
went and told, and loved it. I talked to
Satori at the faculty club, he warned me
there were no paintings. "Just a lot of
stuff," he said. What are we doing?—

killing them again? How did anything
survive the Bolsheviks! As in the famous
Auden poem, there are always those not
taken with the tragedy, who will not be
reformed. The sentimentalists among us,
those who would try to save the past.
I see them, close to tears, running
around the palace, 1917, scooping up a
dress, a doll, a handful of lace. Oh
those sins were real, and yet what joy,
what dreams were here. Tchaikovsky's
music at Christmas, the lost world.
(I think it's at The Lied again, for
The Holidays.) I play the little game
we all play—who would I have been?
Put on two or three garments, sneak out
through the hordes. Then we come into the
treasure room. I move close to pearled
robes, such intricate work—like looking
close at Van Gogh, the tortured energy gone
deep into each twist of paint. The pearls
are all misshapen. I think
of Byzantine ceramics, Yeats, entranced
and sailing to Byzantium. The glue that
sticks the fractured tiles together—
what is it?—longing? love? hope?
I am not a seamstress but a woman lives in
me. She is soothed in the soft light of
the exhibit rooms—still shaking from
miles of snow. And once, turning south
on US 75, the car ahead of us, like a snowy

barn, stopped. Someone inside, old perhaps,
frazzled, could go no further. Russia is
a vast country. The Czar calls to us across
his snowy wastes. His citizens, his countrymen,
we yield to the call of The Father.
We only can obey. Puccini under these
conditions is transformed. Hot voices
and the heater pushed full blast keeps the
ice off the windshield. Four times, though,
I went out battered by sleet, I could have
used one of those sable hats Nicholas looked
so good in, or the tall furred thimbles
of the Cossacks—Barb's famous "Russian
dancers" every Christmas in "The Nutcracker."
How we cling to the past. In "The New Yorker"
article, this fall, the one I couldn't put
down, they shot The Czar and all his children,
Anastasia too, pointblank in the cellar,
then dragged them up the stairs, some still
alive. Bullets fired close up did not kill them
on account of jewels sewn into garments, held
then close to the heart. Standing there,
Topeka, Friday night, looking at a glass case
with a crown inside, I can't forget. Beauty is
innocent. The convulsions of history cannot
destroy it all. In one case, a robe, three
hundred years old, looks almost new.
No bullet holes or blood stains. If we
could get inside their minds, past language,
beyond fear, there would be this eye, this
pink gemstone, large and crude, uncut,

atop the crown—and my hand reaching
out. I picked up pebbles on the beach
in Erie, the summer Barb and I were married.
In the waters of the lake, newly restored,
they held their colors chill and pure. On the
windowsill later, drying out, turned common,
pale and dull. Like anything.
But here they are again, clasped in gold
crimps, under the deep green light of the
past. It was a dream we went on, drove off
into. Driving on off into time, into a Russian
blizzard. "Treasures of the Czars." Come down
to the here and now. The past lives! As from
my father's father I preserve in me the snowy
wastes. I am of good peasant stock. During the
winter months, we who have bent our backs in
his fields all summer begin to straighten,
begin to rise! November I am almost risen now.
Unkinked from the cramped car, it takes a while
for us not to stagger. Now we come to The Czar's
palace. It is flat now, modest, in keeping
with our new socialist values. The guards
have given way inside to cheery women
in white blouses, peasant fashion, who
drape, over our shoulders, like a bag or
purse, our own personal tour guides.
Now we can be alone with our thoughts,
as we must have wanted. Now we begin
our tour of the vast chambers. Silver
and gold, silver at the core with gilt over
it, the surface etched or carved. It has that

brass look of cheap trinkets from India,
advertized as brass but really
some base metal plated. My "brass"
candles rusted on the shelf of our humid
basement. I know how objects fail, get
lost, dispersed, taken to the dump.
Everything dissolves in the acids of
time. The bath of our busyness. The
rain of our daily weather to erase my
hands, your touch, the memory of your
face. Where is The Czar? Where are the
children to animate these dolls? Where
are the laughter and the tears. Pearls
bent and writhing like maggots adorn the
sacred garments. Large chill teardrop
gems protrude from gold cheeks of crowns,
as if frozen there from our last weeping.
Meaning is a sharing of object and function,
use and dream. These artifacts revert towards
color and design, become abstract. They might
well be illusions on a screen, images
lodged in a poem. We went out
from there to the gift shop, America's
answer to everything—love, disaster,
the ends of empires. Shelves covered
with stack dolls in hideous black and
red, the cheap glare of lacquer. We
couldn't find a thing to buy. Drained,
feeling poor, we had come so far to
find The Czars, had we not? But there
was no one there. We made our way to

a small hovel beside the highway, a
place called Shoney's with a glaring sign,
the neon lacquer of the proletariat.
We ate bad soup and salad out of crude
bowls, as if we had regressed, gone back
toward the cave. And had become quite
homeless here, no place to stay in all
Topeka, all the inns closed against the
weary travelers. As in The Christmas
Story once, set against another myth of
empire, another lost civilization crumbling
down into its artifacts. Yet we were joyous.
Six hours in the car and then
that glitter in our eyes had dazzled us.
Barb on the phone all over town, looking
for a place to stay. A strange man
came to our rescue. A blue statue at the
door when we came in, in the uniform of some
system, and wearing a gun at his waist,
installed at Shoney's over the salad bar. The
Czars all dead, and nothing
left to save, free us toward new purposes.
There he was from out of nowhere, and sat
among us and heard our plight. Our common
laughter rose as one. Giddy from lack of
sleep, we told our story. Jody was
delightful, Echo's first husband Paul's
bright sister, in whose eyes and speech
the human spirit shone. Perhaps she is
the lost child everybody's looking for?
All around the table majesty moved, first

Cindy in the spotlight like some princess,
loved and nursed and taught at great expense,
then giving way to me, then Echo goofy,
happy like she always is, Jeff's deep
voice gave depth and resonance to our
sad opera. Barb was hilarious, kept
drawing out our guest, and once he
almost doubled over laughing, breaking
through whole centuries of reserve. All
our phony lacquer shattered, all our tears
were real. His name is Romero Salinas,
one of Topeka's finest. And offered up
his house for us to sleep—to be our
palace at the journey's end. There he
was, our little Nicholas, dressed in his
proper uniform, protector of the realm,
whose vigilance presides over our sleep.
His blue shirt shone with polished brass
like gold. In his voice, distant, you
could hear the ghost of another tongue,
unlearned through time. So the Czar came and
sat at our table. Barb's rings flashed and
glinted, earrings flickered like rare
candle flames, white teeth flashing, as if
polished by the words of our delight.
So we joined present and past, place and
time. We had found the treasures of
the Czars.

NIGHTCRAWLERS

We were not farmers yet we gathered,
nights, beneath the moon, the lawn wet
from the sprinklers, father out ahead,
wearing his miner's lamp strapped
around his forehead, the battery pack
clamped to his waist, the long thin
wire leading down, to have both hands
free, or one to hold the bucket filled
with leaves, one hand for reaching.
Or I would come behind to bring the
bucket, father up ahead, bent down
in his famous crouch over the dirt,
snagging them, snaring them, lifting them
up in loops, to turn and hand them back
to me. "Here's a good one," he might
say, under his breath, barely audible,
then still himself before
that fatal lunge. Or "Shit, I missed
him!"—then to get more intense, so
he would not slip back and lose his
touch, until our backs from being bent
might never straighten, then we would
come to the sidewalk's grained face—
looking so close I'd see the pebbles
there, and know that everything had
something else inside, a little baby
of the new world yet to be born.

Then we might rise and stand and he would
heft the bucket, saying "Good," then light
a cigarette. Strange harvest, out of the
earth come, and might get
two in one if where he reached two
worms had come together, lying side
by side, as I guessed people did.
To make the new child in the dark.
How did they find each other in the
night? I asked him once, and looked
to see them stretching in the dark,
one end still encased in the shaft
and safety, back down to the earth
again, the other on its mission in
the grass. He showed me how to put
the beam of the light below me at my
feet, and let the dimmer circle drift
ahead, like a wave in the lake ahead
of us as we walk. The bright and
concentrated beam would scare them,
but the dimmer light, which was just
bright enough for us to see, if we
looked hard, disclose them in their
slippery sheen. I was repelled at
first, when, out fishing, my worm
came off the hook and father had to
put the next one on, afraid to touch
them or to catch a fish, hoping I
would not catch one. I had two
wishes, both of them the wishes of
a coward, not to have a bite at all—

I never told him this—but not to lose
the worm either, so I might cast all
day, and never have another care. But
then I learned to love them. We would
crouch together side by side, like
women giving birth in the old way,
and he would hand me the flashlight,
then show me how the two hands
worked, in unison, the rim
edge of the light leading
the hand, or the hand drifting as
the light flowed behind it. It
was hard to tell which end was
which, both ends seemingly free,
though one was often in the earth
for sudden exits from the surface
world. And might grab the free
end by mistake, and could not hold
it. You had to grab the part
just at the hole, to cut off its
escape, forgetting the longer part
that lay behind, concentrating on the
inch or so that hugged the walls of
the shaft. And not pull hard right
off or I would break them,
but coax them out, a tiny portion
at a time. They were fitted with
rings of fiber, bands around the
outside just below the skin, and
so when stretched would use these
rings to grab the dirt walls, making

them hard to pull. The proper
motion was like fishing, tugging
on the line a while, then holding
up, while keeping the tension taut,
then to reel in some more. Until,
exhausted, they yielded, worm or fish,
and you could take them in your hands.
First the lawn had to be mowed. We'd
start way back and early in the day,
so as not to have grass too thick,
wherein we could not find them. Then
put the sprinklers out, a half an hour
on each piece, then move them to the
front perhaps, both sections just
inside the hedge. Then wait for
nightfall. We were like vampires or
werewolves, waiting for the moon to
shine, and had to still ourselves, not
walk with heavy feet upon the earth.
They were all skin, and sensitive, without
eyes to see, but would know us when we
came. So was the harvest made. Some
nights we might be out an hour, or we
might start too soon before they had
emerged, then to go back inside to
wait in the kitchen and talk of
aimless things. Come both together
like that in perfect unity, working
toward some common good,
the weekend looming, the Saturday
morning trip to the stream our goal.

"Good, we have enough now," he would
say, standing up, hefting the pail.
Out of the dirt come and our bent
backs, in labor like the centuries
of those before us, crawling near
the earth, beauty uplifted came,
the magic trout, elusive in the
riffles of the stream. He taught
me how to cast the worm upstream,
letting the natural drift bring it
down, in front of all the wary and
difficult fish, and not to flail the
water which might tear the worm,
but rather loft it gently, letting
it land soft. I got so good I
could use the same worm for hours,
re-hooking it maybe shorter or
longer, putting the barbed part
through a new clear untorn section,
then send it out again. He taught me
not to bunch the worm together on
the hook, looking like a knot, but
to let both ends dangle deliciously,
and make a natural motion in the
water, the way a worm would, washed
in miles upstream, begin its long
wild journey to the sea. There was an
art to everything, a time in
the affairs of men, a tide that
pulled us too. In the current of
the stream you felt it, from out

of the cold north, a shower of ice-melt
downward through the trees,
and would have a tough time crossing
on the slippery rocks. He taught me
how to wedge my feet between the
rocks, and not to set my foot down
full and flat upon a slab of slate,
and to lean into the current so as to
have some giving room if I lost
my footing. Or we would cut a walking
stick when the river was high, and
let it lead us all the way across,
like the white cane of the blind
feeling the way. Worms were not
pretty. Their writhing on the hook
bespoke their agony, and made me
sorry, but then to cast them all the
way across, right against the dark
green run against the bank, dropping
them in just right as my breath
stuck in my throat. They were
living things, unlike the artificial
lure or fly, which some say are
superior, and I read a book on
fishing once where every other page
someone's making fun of what we
did—who "drowned a worm" to catch
a trout. To me it seemed the
perfect thing, the perfect combination
of the made and found, like poetry
itself, good fortune and skill,

and "reading" the water, a living
thing to lure a living thing, our
agent in the flurry of the stream,
as if my hand reached out, two
fingers dangling, doing my little
walk along the pebbles. We caught
a lot of trout, and Dad would put
them in his creel, an odd and lovely
basket formed to fit along his hip,
so as to not be in the way. Along
the stream he showed me how to
find the ferns, upgathered,
unfurling dark and green and beautiful.
In this net we'd lay the trout, like
jewels in silk or velvet, silk and
velvet themselves, a speckle of many
colored spots along their sides,
I think that I could look at one
all day and never see enough.
Might catch one early and lay it
down and then sit down beside it
to look at it before the colors
faded, or lay them in my own creel,
on top of a layer of fern, a
fish, then more ferns, and then
another trout, this one longer
maybe, this one fatter, this one maybe
a different kind, a rainbow with its
broad pink stripe, a "brown" with its
murky look. We labored
in the dark for this. Bent over

like barbarians, cave dwellers over
some dark feast, and then to stand
up tall and living in the light, fifty
thousand years beyond. To trade our
muddy fingers for the quick flash of
the trout in icy water, sudden zigzag
of the struck fish, upstream crazy in
the current, swimming hard right at it,
trying to unhook itself, or might leap
out from the very depths, shaking
its great and massive head, in
order to throw off the hook.
Then tear off with the flow,
threatening to strip all the line
from my reel. What could compare?
To touch my fingertips against the
line and catch the telegraph the
worm was sending me, of snags and
twists along the unseen depths,
a branch to catch on or a rock to
scrape, so I could read the bottom
of the stream like Braille—and
then the jagged strike. So would
we lay the worms out gently on the
grass beside the stream, kneeling
in the great church of the new pink
morning, and he would divide them each
to each, four or five smaller ones,
perfect as they were, and to each a few
monsters, which would come in handy
later for breaking into parts, checking

them over for health and vitality,
discarding all sickly or limp ones,
until we had our full complement, then
toss in a handful of dirt and leaves
into the green worm box. Then
would we rise in the new
morning, brush ourselves off,
or bend and wipe the worm slime from
our hands, then head out walking
into the roar of the stream. We
fished fast-moving water. It was
the only way. Degrees of pretension, as
we were not fit company for the dry fly
man, so did we think ourselves
superior to all those sleeping ones
along the pond side, bobber-fishing
in the heat of midday, coolers of
beer at their feet. And would get
up in the dark to load our gear,
and have that one last swig of coffee
before setting out, then drive ten
miles into the hinterlands. Dad had a
favorite spot, Twin Bridges, off
blacktop onto gravel we went, and then
to dirt, throwing up a plume of dust
behind us. Perhaps to arrive,
to be the first ones there, then
slip our heavy boots on, traipse
on down through the cow pasture.
Fish Creek broadens there, beneath
the bridges, but splits, forcing

the double bridge, comes on both
wide and fast, green in the dawn, gold
later, the water colors changing, dark
over dark rocks, bright in the
shallows, silver where the water
whitened. Or always it seemed,
just out of reach of my cast, the
deepest run where all the lunkers
lay. Every day was new, like life
itself, a perfect metaphor for what
we lived all week, but more intense,
more life and death between us.
Taking the fish themselves into
our bodies, the very fabric of the
earth into ourselves, to fill my
sleep with images. And then to
wake and go there. How many times
we went I do not know, enough to
print the place eternal in my mind,
and I could take you there I think,
from memory still. He had gone
there alone before I was born, and
I would take my son there after my
father's death. To work upstream
to where Alder Creek joined the
other, in that spring torrent, to
toss our shining lures into the
very teeth of the torrent. To
catch no fish—maybe we should
have been using worms! Where
father laughed and straightened from

his crouch, and held one up, long as a
snake from his strenuous battle, and
lit a cigarette with trembling hands.
There was so much to know. And passed
on to me the old bamboo fly rod in
three sections, so thin and strong, but
yet which magnified the actions of the
fish so anything I caught seemed
powerful, and which might pull me in,
yank my very heart out of my chest. And
taught me how to form the fishing knot,
with a loop through the loop again, to
snug the line against itself for
holding. And taught me how to run the
ferrules through my hair to grease them
before joining, so later they would come
apart, and taught me how to put the rod
behind my back, and pull my arms
apart so as not to bend the rod
unduly and snap it, letting the
body's natural grace, even in this
unruly figure, guide the path
to separate the portions. He was all
knowledge, everything I needed, and
there I was teaching my son
last week the stroke on the tiny
pond, and thought of my father's
beam of light in the darkness,
leading me along, reaching back
to pass the bounty. In deep woods
I see him out along the stream

where he has gone in search of ferns
to line the fishing basket. Or
high on South Inlet, following the fast
water up, a little further year by
year, then come to the old power dam
with the big pool in front of it, I
remember that morning how he shouted
that he "had a good one" and helped him
land it, holding the bent wood of the
trout net under the thrashing fish—then
took his picture—boy was he proud! Or
there he goes now with the walking
stick in the full rage of spring runoff,
edging out, sliding his feet
along the gravel, or wedging
in between the rocks, making his
slow journey towards—what?—
that distant shore, some wild idea
of casting in along that far bank
that we never reach, where the big
ones lay like submarines, mossed
over in the deep water. By eye
we spied them in their realm and
inky depths, or watched them skim
like birds on the other side of
that film which joins the worlds,
or reached out with our hands to
lift them thrashing from the net,
and hear them speak the silence
of the wilderness. His grandson now
has taken up the art of fishing,

loves it, though he can't say why,
has taken over all the gear, and has
it stowed in the trunk of his car,
along with life vests and canoe
paddles, dreams of the wilds of
Colorado, and will call me no doubt
late from some toll phone, high
off a mountain road. Uses
the new rubber worms, made of some
infinitely brilliant plastic,
firm and elastic at once, to shimmer
all their colors in the local ponds. I
went with him last year to Yankee
Hill, and watched him cast his
favorite purple worm amongst the lily
pads and weeds, and hook the mighty
fish out of the depths. And are called
back, each child of us back
to the earth and to the water out
of which we come, forgetful yet
the tide that pulls our hearts,
the current carries us away, and we
will stand there but a little while,
and then we let go and are gone.

THE PEN ELEC SITE

for Stanley Lantz

My heart would race whenever I would hear
the names. Tenochtitlan, Xochimilco, Machu
Picchu, cities of the sun. And I would imagine
done there things beyond knowing, things
beyond our patience or wisdom,
as if they had gone so far into nightmare they
could not come back, then to let their cities
die. I could come home and sit
in my chair, feet up, and open to
the pages of the "Geographic," there to be
appalled, warriors with huge feather bonnets,
giant wooden clubs hardened in the fire,
saw-toothed edges, a high stockade,
a narrow bridge to span the moat,
and in the moat below the bridge
the tangles of the slain. Re-creations
they have told us, artists' renderings
from out of the ruins. What did they
live to do? What was the point of it all?
Then, in another issue, from out of a
green blanket, the first scrapings
where a wall comes down into a shallow pit,
a staircase covered with murals,
beautiful flowers, beautiful women,
figures done in profile, each with that cruel
and sculptured nose, nostrils flaring, as

if an animal had learned to paint,
had learned to sing. Their instruments of
music would engage me, narrow flutes—
and one made from a human bone, a tibia,
with holes bored in the top, their fingers
placed so carefully along the shin—
what to be thinking then?—lost melodies.
The weight of the lost would stop me,
almost my breath die in my chest.
There in those glittery pages I would look
wide-eyed as if I had gone back in time.
Borne of compassion, awe and fear,
a terror grip me—I would sit there late,
Barb gone to bed, until I could bear
to look no more and closed the book.
Pen Elec was like that, some coded name,
something that does not come across
into our language, some Mayan dialect
or dying scream, beyond translation. A
deep jungle ride, a river ride, upstream,
against the flow as against the river of
time itself, backtracking towards
the source and where we came from.
They told me he was "over there,"
working the site all year now.
No one had seen him—oh there were rumors
around Warren, then when Jack and Claire
stopped, two or three times, always the house
closed up, the cat on the porch bereft.
And pour a little water in its dish.
He was a wild one. Jack told how he and Stan

would walk the Kinzu Bridge, the highest in
the world, waiting for the train to come, and
when it did they draped themselves
over the rails as the whole bridge shook.
That's how they made their fun. How once
Stanley had climbed straight down, two hundred
feet, in and out of the huge girders, above
the tiny trickle of the stream—
no more than a thread below. And I could
barely walk where they walked, given my
chance—I started out and got half way, turned
back, unable to open my eyes. Two wild kids
they were—then off to War to give
the Japs hell. For years he'd kept
the family house, but didn't live there,
spent all his time digging the valley sites
around Mt. Jewett, was called in by the
state commission when they built the great
Kinzu Dam. Then he'd dug the sites along
the river as they brought the dozers in—
every time they'd blade a pile of rubble over
and a few points, some artifacts, there
was Stanley in his shirtsleeves, pencil
behind an ear. I had always favored him
among the long-lost relatives on that side,
scattered near and far. Stanley remained for
me a natural force, something like a good
hard rain to turn the gravel over
and disclose the bones. Ten years back it
was when he came through and stopped at
Jack's, and took a beer with us. I was his

welcoming committee, full of questions,
all so new to me. For others more the
same old thing, like cutting meat, the
way they made their living. I remember
that look in his eye, Stanley sketching pots,
showing the slender lines of the throats,
the globes of the bellies. Here was 1250,
the way they bunched the clay, and here, a
hundred miles away, two hundred years
later—he made a little flourish with his
wrist, the pots got taller, prettier. He
knew everything, knew what they ate,
knew what their houses looked like,
knew how they built their stockades,
had found the post holes marking their
perimeter, and finding one, knew where
to dig to find the next one—and did
me a drawing showing the whole encampment,
the river racing by below. They would build
by a river, it was so obvious,
I guess, the whole country pure then
in those days, unburned, the rivers running
clear with trout. What did it mean, this
culture lost to us, what could they
tell us now, some secret that they know,
and keep from us—is it because we
burned them out? Polluted their streams?
Could I know it if I tried? This
nausea I felt, awaking to the savage past,
was it the beast in me? He loved his work.
I had never seen someone show such

reverence for the dirt beneath our feet.
He showed me how to tell one culture
from another, laying his hand over the
slope of the pot. I think he could have
talked the night away. And then he
disappeared. He drank his beer, got up
and left, and left his sacred drawings
on the table top. And then he was gone
off into remote centuries, with no one
hearing any news, until he'd suddenly
turn up, haggard and dirty, sprawl in
somebody's kitchen, put his lovely
sketches on some napkins. He got
conflated in my mind with Kurtz,
off in his dark interior, the final
outpost, there to partake of who knew
what? Something only the blood knows.
Years we did not see him or hear a
word. Then he was over "there" at
"Pen Elec." I needed to go. One day
the four of us went down, Jack driving,
Claire in front riding shotgun, Barb
and I in back. They told us Stanley
was expecting us. Down through the rolling
countryside we went, green grown all
around us—I went into my jungle past.
Outside the car the blur of trees, that
fragile feeling sitting in the back,
remembering all those hours down to
Nani's house, how I would lie on the
window ledge in back and watch the

world spin past. Drowsy, sleeping,
the aching rumble of the car there
in my bladder, waking up to pee.
It was like that going down to
Pen Elec. All the way down I
imagined the place, was not good
company, had gone dark deep inside
myself, stood with the shadows of time,
remembering the Plath poem, "It was
a place of force," narrow ledge
of the dream. I saw there lovely
arbors hung with fruits, herds of
strange beasts, and then around their
fires, in the glint of the coals, the
glint and glare of sparkling eyes.
Then we were there. "Here it is,"
Jack said driving down the hill.
Gigantic smokestacks loomed against
the sky, the way perhaps at Auschwitz
they had stood, the Yard surrounded by a
heavy fence, barricades along the road,
and further back huge buildings.
A guard at the gate stopped us,
as I peered out from in the back
a child again, to peer through the
smudged window, sweated with my
breath. Jack said the password
and we were allowed. Through some
fantastic yard we went, great hoops
of wire, gigantic spools, huge terminals,
great bonnets of steel and insulators like

barbaric hairdos of the Incas
or the Aztecs, sent through me ecstatic
shudders. We took a dirt trail through
the Yard out back where the
pavement ended and the grass began ,
a wide landscape of weeds. There beside the
river now disclosed a humble shack or
rather shop front like the fake fronts of
some western town or movie set,
and there was Stanley in his jungle garb.
Another man was with him tending a pump
and a dredge hose. Water from the river
gushed from its end like spurting blood
out of the jugular. They had a kind
of trellis set above a cement channel
cut in the bank, and racks of screens
filled with the gravel set there to be
washed. Below the screens the muddy
water ran back to the river, to leave
behind the tiny bits of rock—or
whatever the hell it was Stanley was
looking for. He fitted us with trowels
and brushes. Off to the left, not far
from where we'd parked the car, pieces
of ground staked out into the fashion of
a grid, each one numbered. Into each box
he placed each one of us. There was
just enough room to squat or
sit, as if around a fire long ago,
just inside the cave mouth. A bucket
each to put our dirt in, then we set

to work. The sky was overcast.
We would scrape gently over the hard
compacted soil, drawing the blade of
the trowel towards us, then lift the
dirt to the bucket. I never looked so
hard at the earth. Barb in pit 7,
I in 8, an hour passed. Or two. We were
looking for beads, tiny red and blue and
other-colored beads, which Stanley said
their culture had acquired in trade with
whites. He was especially happy if
we found one. Then Barb found a
large smooth stone embedded in the
earth, and brushed around it, bringing
it up more and more. It was a small
stone ax, with one end broken off.
I was amazed. Stanley seemed
unimpressed. He had this way about
him, this long patience. He had been
there—what?—three years already,
though nobody would ever think so.
Little had been done, it seemed, only
an inch or two of soil had been removed,
the site gone off in all directions.
Trying to stand my legs were
stiff and cramped. Such is the life
of the glamorous archaeologist. All
day we worked, not wanting to give up,
I felt the river chill come up the
bank, the breeze through our hair.
When we finished we took a look at

his stuff, huge notebooks filled with
grids and drawings, tiny sketches
marked on every page, shards and beads
depicted in great detail, the finest
pen point and the blackest ink, bone
black or the soot of ancient trees.
We had built up good appetites, for
all our helplessness. Ever cheerful, joyous
even, in the face of the immensity of his
task, what I would call monotony of
all the years behind him and
the years to come, he seemed
to me a strange and wondrous man,
hair blowing in the wind, one of the
wise old fathers, Stanley himself the
one sure thing worth saving
down at Pen Elec. Back in the car,
out of the wind, we rode with our
own thoughts back. Our silence partly of
humility, partly embarrassment,
and sadness too. Jack drove a while,
and no one spoke. I sat in the back
my hands in my lap, those useless hands,
then absent-mindedly I lay my fingers
on the graceful metal of the handle of
the door—smooth, a shiny chrome—
which will "turn up" some day perhaps
beneath the trowel—some
summer kid up out of Pittsburgh or
Carnegie Mellon, then call out to some
future century's Stanley Lantz,

who will then class and name it—
"Chevrolet"—the "big Caprice,"
early nineties, "Standard stuff though
quite a decent specimen at that."
If anybody cares to look at all.

THE KNIFE WITHOUT A HANDLE THAT NEVER HAD A BLADE

It was one of my father's favorite sayings.
I don't know where it comes from. Oh
I could look it up, somebody knows, but
maybe I don't care. Write me if you know.
He said it often, I forget the contexts. Maybe
it did not make sense. Something about
being useless, the way I was, wasn't I?
Or maybe it was just something to say,
the way a father is supposed to have
something to say. The world not slip
past unnoticed, unremarked upon.
He was full of these choice sayings.
Most of them enigmatic, most of them
slightly sardonic, or self effacing.
He was never enthusiastic about anything.
I have his photo on my desk right now,
at twenty, maybe, a sober look, not a trace
of a smile. Looking like he hadn't smiled
at all, not even once. The mouth
straight across, the teeth concealed.
The eyes sad. How far could you go
with this face? How many doors could
be opened with this look? How many
people charmed? Not many. I asked
my mother in a letter just the other day
to tell me what it was she saw in him,

or what he'd been like—different somehow,
from the man I knew. What was he like
young, how did he start to get old?
We are responsible for each other.
I need to take him by the arm and
sit him down, and show him how to
write a poem. I needed to go and
stand with him in his shop, and let
the sawdust fall on me, until I was
covered with it, then let him brush
me off. Then tore the letter up. I do not
want to know, or it cannot be known,
or I would rather pick my way through the
fragments, taking each one in turn, to
read the mystery there. The way each
thing we do goes back before time,
the poem into the hand, the hand back
into the claw, the claw back into the fin,
the fin back into the lobe, and then
into the bulge, and then into the cell,
the waters still, the sun pouring down.
He was a strange one, I will tell you.
I will tell you all I know of him, but
each in turn, in increments, a little at
a time, as he was himself patience personified,
like a cave column forming from a
single drip down from the roof. Let
me not rush things. He wouldn't have.
He would have these funny things
to say, I started to remember them
the other night. I plan to keep thinking.

Maybe I can bring them back. He was
a patient thinker in the world.
Something would occur, then he would try
his words, learning what life offered,
then finding words for it. He made
me in his image, his son, his offshoot,
his betrayer, my whole life squeezed down
into words, like this. Before the poem
that springs up fresh in my throat,
like a song or shout, there was the
hand to write, there was the throat,
the tongue shaping words. Before that his
hand reached out, and the stove hot, and
the heat on his fingertips, the
shout of pain. Back before that there
were the objects tilting towards the
light, cells collecting on the surface
of the sea, warmed by the sun, and then
the lobe emergent, reaching upwards
towards the light. He was my first teacher.
Dumb as a rock, I would take the
files he left out on the bench for me,
and drive them in like chisels into
stones, and break the tips off his scrapers,
ground sharp for scraping paint off wood.
I perverted his tools, not even learning
their names. He was my first poet,
showing me within his mouth the shape
of pain, the meaning that the day became,
all that light and rain dispersed
and gathered up into the peonies against

the fence. Once I helped him fix the car. It
was the 49 Chevy, I think, the dark green one,
so lovely, I can still see it coming down
Schuyler Street. He lay on the
floor in the garage, with a tarp under
him, no walker, so that he had to wiggle
along, lifting a shoulder, stretching
a little, gaining a little ground, then
lifting the other to pull himself along.
I can still remember seeing his feet
going in, under the car. I would hand
him tools. His arm would come out,
or his hand, and he would say "Give me
the wrench," and I would hand him
something and he would say, "Not that
one," and give it back to me. His voice
so far away, his whole attention directed
elsewhere, then I would look again over
the assembled tools, and try to guess
which one he wanted. I was
no good at it. Or holding the light. He
had me try that too, a few times, standing
beside him, up on tip toes, reaching over
the fender of the car, focusing the light
upon some rusted bolt or knot of grease,
which he signaled was his object. And
would lose my concentration almost right
away, the light drifting off, then he
would stop whatever he was doing, prying,
twisting, and I would be singing or
daydreaming, until, at last, not sensing

any movement from him, I would turn my
gaze upon him. And he would be standing
there looking at me. Was
this the evolution from the fish?
And the green cell that sprouted limbs
and climbed up onto the land, there
to learn farming and to love music.
What was he evolving into? He might
wonder then, he might well wonder.
Long ago the soul began its journey.
First the slime shook in the sun,
clustering and knotting like grease
on a bolt under the hood of the car. And
God or something put its wrench upon the
grease and found the bolt within, and
turned the bolt. And I was there, with
the light gone splayed across the
sky of the uplifted hood
of the Chevy, parked in his garage,
singing my little songs. And the slime
got up on its feet and walked. My
father was born in New York City,
Whitestone, a small town on Long
Island. His mother and father
had two houses, and I ran my hand along
the wall of the stucco of his mother's
house, while riding my bike, and carry
the scar still. At the end of his arm
the slime had assembled itself into
the claw of the hand, which then
not serving well would

take unto itself various tools, made
of steel, wrenches and pliers. Out in
one shed out back I found one
day the race car Father built—
an amazing thing. He could do most
anything with steel. I found his
diving helmet in the attic of the
old garage, and wish I had it now,
to put on the desk or hang on the
wall, a strange contraption, built
out of his longing for what he'd
left behind a hundred million years—
and would go back into the sea again,
looking for some clue perhaps to
what it had intended once. We came
ashore, and landed on Long Island,
hundreds of millions of years ago,
and squirmed inland by putting one lobe
up, the way my father wedged himself up
under the car, lifting one shoulder up,
like an amoeba, pulling the rest behind.
And came to that hill above the
houses where they lived, and
slid a little down the hill—
the house he was born in was about
halfway down—and built itself
a home there. They were all patient
then. Each morning was a thousand
years, and Poppa would go off to
work, and pour cement, and let it
dry, and pour some more, then come on

home and pour some whiskey in a
glass, then go to work, ten thousand
years, they went like this. Poppa was
original, spoke some odd mixture of
languages, a little Ukrainian
out of the dirt of that far region,
and crossed the sea like sunlight
pushing the green ahead of it, and
washed up on the shore, and put
its funny elbows down and walked.
I remember him late in his life,
he understood the movement of the sun,
and Helen, his daughter, would always talk
of Poppa and his garden—he would be out
there scraping the earth with some claw
grown out of his arm, but spoke
in sighs and groans, or turned away
when he didn't understand, nor sang
at all, nor wrote a single poem.
In his bedroom drawer he kept the
whiskey bottles with the fire of the
sun within the slime to fire him, then
he might sigh and swear, sigh and
groan, then pour a little more
light into his glass. Ten thousand
years the amber liquid shook, until
my father poured himself a glass,
and drank, and uttered his fine
phrases. One of his favorites was
this one about the knife. That was
without a handle, lacking as well

a blade. And he would say it with
sadness, as if much had ended
there with this knowledge, as if
much fond hope had come to little
there. Was he talking about me? I
never knew. Was he given perhaps
one chance to look upon the evolution
from the fish, and make some comment?
There I stood beside him, letting
the light from the flashlight spray
upon the firmament of the hood of the
car. And left him in the dark. What did
it mean? How might it guide me still?
I remember that the knife
was not merely a metaphor, how he
kept knives near him, one in his pocket,
one close at hand always. He was always
finding things to do with knives, and
worked in fact in a machine shop next to
The Knife Plant at Oneida
Limited, the silverware company.
And they would come to hunger in
the flesh, and they would reach
their lobes out to embrace the world,
and take it in, until their hands
took proper instruments, in index
of their evolution's proper reach.
Poppa ate with his hands, I recall,
the huge fingers, the monstrous
thumb like some numb appendage
groping in the slime. My favorite

image of him he's at the dining table
with his thumb covered in mashed
potatoes, looking up through red
and swollen eyes. My father took
to building knives at home, in his
spare time, and we would draw them
out on paper in advance, then he
would sketch the form on a blank of
steel, then cut it out, and bring
it home. All around me where I sit
the knives are setting on the shelves,
and I have reached my hand and picked up
one, the nearest one, and held it
in my hand. He had, for some reason, an
odd idea about the human hand.
None of the handles fit my grip. I keep
passing my hand over them, trying to get
comfortable, like the fish putting its
lobe out, testing the weight, trying to
walk. I keep moving my hand, trying to
span the whole handle, then bringing the
thumb down, to prop against the guard of
the knife. There is something monumental
about them, all oversized, and one real
monster, it must weigh five or six
pounds, that's not a knife at all, but
some outlandish symbol
of something, I can't think what.
But think of evolution's many stumbles
in the dark, the hands reaching to touch,
reaching to shape, not knowing what it

wants, or where it's going. Was this what we
wanted? He built one for himself, it may
have been the very first he made, then one
for his brother Bill, who carried it for
three years in the Philippines, a large
Bowie style, but functional, I think Bill used
it, though he never said, but wanted it
back, after Dad died, and came in
and told me; I was sitting in the room,
and I remember picking it up, and
handing it to him, the handle fit
my hand. It was a knife possessed both
of a blade and handle, and even had a
sheath. Towards the end of
the flurry of my father's making
he would build knives without sheaths
at all, and even had a few blades in
drawers, roughed out, or one just cut
out of its block of steel, in
silhouette, the work abandoned.
Some blind alley perhaps, of evolution's
march? Where would it go next? What form
would it take? I remember being
on the floor, as if washed up, some early
memory, or else gone back three hundred
million years, as if without legs or
arms, just lying there, as we must all
assemble ourselves out of the slime, first
the cells joining, then the bulge forming,
and the lobes, strange gills out of the
throat, which later will speak poetry,

and the fish sleeps in the mother's
sea, swims in the endless
orb of her womb, walks upon tiny lobes.
If you look at the fetal child where
the hands will be that write the poems
there is for many weeks a pod erupting
from the grease of cells, and then a
kind of lobe, and then a fin, and then
an arm, and then the famous photo where
the child has its thumb in its mouth,
sucking on the breast it does not
yet know. I was not good
with tools. He'd give me the flashlight
and I'd drop it. I remember that—
breaking the bulb. He'd fiddle with it—
his word, not poetry yet, but the lobe of
poetry, stuck out above the slime, something
to put a glove on, or five fingers in which,
early on, the pen might be held, the
sonnet practiced. Nothing he made
fit me. Young, I could not
get my hand around the grip, or
know what purpose was served. The
knives were archaic, some throwback—
his word!—some ancient slippage of
our progress, where memory slides
backwards into the past. Once, I think,
some ancestor had need of such a
blade, had blood on his mind, or wood
to split. We see the physical self
shrinking as we come forward, the

head growing larger, the body gone
in atrophy, the muscles withering.
Once, ten thousand years ago, my
father's father's father's father's
father could not speak at all, not
even a sign, but took some tool like this
and killed a man. It was a terrible time,
and in that flurry of response was forged
the idea of the knife. It lasted, printed
again and again in the minds of the
cells, grown outward in the world, and
one might wake to find, beside the bed,
a knife with handle and a
blade, but no danger,
and wonder how it got there. So
was my father one of these, these
throwbacks towards the dawn, a blood
red sun in the sky. There was no use for
these knives, except to look at them.
Except to marvel at their use, and what
became of us, refined through all the
dawnings of eternity. I have them
now, as artifacts, some eloquent yet
numb testimony to the urgency of
blood, and the lobe reaching out,
becoming the hand. But what of
this strange artifact of his speech,
this enigmatic phrasing set against
the pressure of time? Surely some
thing badly made, or ill conceived. As
he might once have turned to look at

me, and saw the end of all his work.
There he was, down
on the floor of the garage, wriggling
like sperm in its mad search, while
I, his strange assistant, some
mutant thing, sprayed the light all
over everything. He was in the
dark, where I left him, where some
crazed impulse told me to. I broke
his heart, I think, for failing him
so much. So are the fathers left
behind, like horseshoe crabs washed up
upon that beach in Delaware, I saw them
four years back, these ancient things,
huge bulging foreheads, tiny eyes, and
the long tail thrashing
in the sea, a blade to cut or steer
by. Blind, I suppose, in their love
ecstasy, would crawl up on the shore,
and recapitulate our ancient quest,
now perishing. I had to bring one
home, and hang it on the wall,
souvenir of some journey I'm still
on. How was the transfer made,
out of the slime? As he worked,
my father, with the wrench on the bolt
in the grease, his offspring formed in
his throat a song. Daydreams flashed in
my head, of things undone, of all
things yet to find. And, though my hand
had grown its fingers, I had lost my

grip to hold the light firm. This was
why he lost his faith in me. In
the last years of his life
he did not even speak his phrases. They
had passed to me. I remember going
among his tools after his death. I
went down in the cellar and walked
around. It was like a museum from
fifty million years ago. All that
was missing was the horseshoe crab,
or a bottle perhaps of the original
elixir, out of which everything has
come. I touched the steel of
his tools with great sadness, knowing I
could not go back, knowing I would not
even know their use. And the anger
arising, out of which they came, I had
forgotten even that. I reached my hand
and took the blade of the knife setting
on his bench, and when
I touched the steel a song rose,
magically out of the throat of my
mind. This is that song, lumbering on
ungainly limbs to stand in its place in the
sun. What does it mean? Where are we going?
Oh so far and long.

ABOUT THE AUTHOR

Greg Kuzma has retired from the University of Nebraska-Lincoln as Professor Emeritus after forty-two years of teaching. He taught the writing of poetry at all levels, including graduate courses, but chose to specialize in the beginning course, English 253. He served for thirteen years as the Faculty Advisor to *Laurus*, UNL's fine arts and literary magazine, edited by undergraduates and publishing only undergraduate work. Taking *The New Yorker* as their model, *Laurus* editors published stories and excerpts from novels, poems, book reviews, and essays on film, close readings of books of poems, as well as plays, panel discussions, and graphic art.

Greg lives with his wife Barbara in Crete, Nebraska, twenty-five miles from Lincoln. Barbara was the enrichment teacher for the Crete Public Schools, retiring after thirty-one years. She is an avid tennis player. Their son Mark is a computer programmer for a company out of Chicago. Mark works remotely and is free to locate wherever he chooses, and so has traveled far and wide around the world. Their daughter Jacquelyn and her daughter Alex live in Crete. Jacque teaches English Language Learning. Alex plays the flute and divides her sports time among soccer, basketball, and cross-country.

Greg is presently working with the University Library to establish an archive of his teaching, his poetry, as well as his editorial and publishing career with *Pebble* and The Best Cellar Press.

Mountains of the Moon is the second selection from his longer poems. The first, *All That is Not Given is Lost*, was published in 2007 by the Backwaters Press. A third volume is in preparation.

CPSIA information can be obtained at www.ICGtesting.com
Printed in the USA
LVOW07s2012091013

356208LV00005B/309/P